THE
WORKING
WOMAN'S
COOKBOOK

BY THEODORA ZAVIN & FREDA STUART

Cornerstone Library **New York**

Reprinted 1976

Manufactured in the United States of America
under the supervision of Rolls Offset
Printing Co., New York

Contents

MAIN DISHES

◆◆

☐ BEEF ☐

Boeuf Bourguignon

3 tablespoons salad oil	¼ teaspoon pepper
2 lbs. lean beef chuck, cut in cubes	¼ teaspoon thyme
2 tablespoons flour	1 cup undiluted beef broth
1 teaspoon salt	1 cup Burgundy

1 (3 oz.) can mushrooms	1 small can white onions

The Night Before

Preparation Time: 20 to 25 min.   *Cooking Time:* 2½ hrs.

Heat salad oil in skillet or electric frying pan. Brown meat on all sides. While meat is browning, heat oven to 325°. When meat is browned, stir in flour, salt, pepper, and thyme. Mix well with meat, scraping bottom of pan. Put everything in a 3-quart casserole.

Mix beef broth and wine and pour over meat. Place covered casserole in oven and bake for 2½ hrs. Cool slightly and refrigerate.

Before Serving

Preparation Time: 5 min.   *Cooking Time:* 35 min.

4

Heat oven to 325°. If the liquid has evaporated, broth and wine may be added in equal parts. (This shouldn't be necessary if your oven keeps a proper temperature.) Add drained mushrooms and onions. Stir, cover, and bake for 35 min.

Serves 4

Glazed Corned Beef

3 lbs. corned beef brisket	1 teaspoon salt
1 peeled carrot	Dash of pepper
1 onion, quartered	

. . . .

2 tablespoons prepared mustard	2 tablespoons dark brown sugar
¼ cup maple syrup	

The Night Before
Preparation Time: 10 min.   *Cooking Time:* 3 hrs.

Place corned beef, carrot, onion, salt, and pepper in large saucepan with enough water to cover. Bring to boil and then simmer over a medium flame for 3 hrs. or until beef seems tender. Remove beef from water and let cool. Wrap in foil and refrigerate.

Before Serving
Preparation Time: 10 min.   *Cooking Time:* 18 min.

While broiler is heating, combine mustard, syrup, and brown sugar in a small saucepan. Bring to the boiling point, then reduce heat and simmer for 5 min., stirring frequently. Brush the glazing sauce over the corned beef and put beef in broiler, 5 or 6 inches from heat. Broil for 10 min., brushing two or three times with the remaining glaze. Slice and serve.

Serves 4

Beef Stroganoff

3 tablespoons butter
3 tablespoons flour
2 cups beef broth, boiling

5 teaspoons prepared
 mustard
2 large onions
¼ lb. fresh mushrooms

. . . .

1½ lbs. sirloin, cut in ¼
 inch strips

3 tablespoons butter
6 tablespoons sour cream

The Night Before
Preparation and Cooking Time: 10 min.

Melt butter in a saucepan. Add flour and blend. Add the broth all at one time. Stir and cook until thick. Stir in mustard. Cover and refrigerate sauce.

Slice onions and mushrooms and refrigerate in a plastic bag.

Before Serving
Preparation and Cooking Time: 15 min.

Melt butter in a large skillet (350° if using an electric pan) and saute onions and mushrooms briefly just until they are soft.

Add beef strips and cook briefly until meat is browned on both sides.

While the beef is cooking, reheat the sauce. Add the sour cream and stir until hot but not boiling.

Pour the sauce over the beef mixture in the skillet and serve.

Can be frozen   *Serves 4*

Pot Luck Roast

The glory of this pot roast is in the gravy. And the glory of the gravy is that at some point you're going to run it through your blender so that you can add to it whatever spare vegetables you're hoarding in little dishes in your refrigerator. The few spoonfuls of leftover stringbeans, the one stalk of celery, and/or the half tomato which you toss in do wondrous things for the flavor of the gravy. For your liquid, use water, bouillon or, preferably, any liquid you have saved from canned vegetables. At least ¼ cup of the liquid, however, should be tomato juice, leftover tomato paste, purée, sauce, or what-have-you with a tomato flavor.

If you're short on available preparation time, you can use small canned potatoes and canned whole carrots. If you do, add them when you warm the pot roast before serving.

1 pot roast, about 3 lbs.	1 cup leftover vegetables (see
3 tablespoons salad oil	note above)
1 medium onion, sliced	2 teaspoons flour
2 cups liquid (see note above)	4 potatoes
1 tablespoon salt	1 bunch carrots

The Night Before

Preparation Time: 30 min.   *Cooking Time:* 2½ hrs.

Heat oil in a large pot or Dutch oven. Add onions and cook slowly until golden but not crisp. Add the pot roast and brown it on all sides. Add the liquid, the salt, and the leftover vegetables. Cover and simmer over low flame for 2½ hrs.

While the onions and meat are browning, peel the carrots and potatoes. Cut the potatoes in half and the carrots in thirds. Cook the two vegetables together in boiling water for 20 min. Drain, cool, and refrigerate.

When the meat has simmered the required time, remove it to a plate. Run all the gravy through the blender, adding the flour. (Be careful not to put more gravy into the blender than it can handle at one time. This gravy is too good to waste in spattering or overflow.) You can add a little Kitchen Bouquet or soy sauce for a deeper color if you're so inclined.

Return the gravy and the meat to the pot. Cover and refrigerate.

Before Serving

Preparation Time: 2 min.   *Cooking Time:* 20 min.

Skim fat from gravy. Add carrots and potatoes. Cover and heat over a low flame for 20 min.   *Serves 5 to 6*

Italian Pot Roast

4 lbs. pot roast	1 cup tomato juice
½ teaspoon salt	1 large carrot, sliced
½ teaspoon pepper	2 onions, chopped
2 cloves garlic, cut into slivers	2 teaspoons oregano
½ cup flour	½ teaspoon basil
¼ cup olive oil	1 cup tomato purée

. . . .

3 tablespoons chopped parsley

The Night Before

Preparation Time: 20 min.   *Cooking Time:* 2 hrs.

Rub meat with salt and pepper. Make tiny, deep incisions on all sides of the meat with the point of a knife and push a sliver of garlic into each cut. Roll meat in flour. Heat olive oil in deep, heavy pot and, over high heat, brown meat on all sides. While meat is browning, peel and chop onion, scrape and slice carrot, and measure out other ingredients. When meat is brown, lower heat and add tomato juice, carrot, onion, basil, and oregano. Cover and simmer gently for 1¼ hrs.

After 1¼ hrs., add tomato purée and stir through. Simmer for 45 min. longer. Remove from heat, let stand for 15 min., then refrigerate, covered.

Preparation Time: 3 min.   *Cooking Time:* 20 min.

Discard fat that has congealed on surface of sauce. Place covered pot on top of stove and simmer until meat is hot— about 20 min. Just before serving, chop parsley (if you haven't already done so) and stir into sauce.   *Serves 5 to 6*

Beef Shishkebab

2 lbs. sirloin, cut in cubes
1 large onion, sliced

1 bay leaf
Enough sherry or burgundy to cover

(Use only two of the following. If you plan to use more, you will need 5 skewers for 4 servings.)

½ lb. fresh mushrooms
1 can boiled onions or 2 medium raw onions

3 large tomatoes or 16 cherry tomatoes
2 green peppers

. . . .

4 tablespoons melted butter

The Night Before

Preparation Time: 10 min.

Cover the sirloin cubes with the sliced onion, bay leaf, and wine. Cover the dish and refrigerate.

If you are using mushrooms, wash and stem them. If you are using raw onions, peel them and cut in wedges. Peppers should be washed and cut in 2-inch cubes. Refrigerate the vegetables in a plastic bag.

Before Serving

Preparation Time: 12 min.   *Cooking Time:* 17 to 24 min.

Heat broiler. Melt butter in a saucepan. If you are using fresh tomatoes, cut them in wedges. (Cherry tomatoes, of course, remain whole.) Canned onions should be drained.

Place meat and vegetables on 4 large skewers, alternating pieces. Brush with melted butter. Broil 17 min. if you like your meat fairly rare or up to 24 min. if you like it well done. Turn once halfway through broiling and brush with whatever remaining butter you may have.   *Serves 4*

Chuck Steak Special

This is an ingenious way to make an inexpensive chuck steak taste like something special. Buy enough chuck to feed the number of people you will be serving but use the amounts indicated for the marinade, regardless of the size of the steak. You can, after using it, strain the marinade to remove any meat particles and then refrigerate it for use over and over again.

Chuck steak, cut 2 inches thick,   1 cup dry white vermouth
    well trimmed   ½ cup soy sauce
Unsalted meat tenderizer

The Night Before
Preparation Time: 5 min.

Use meat tenderizer on both sides of steak in accordance with directions on the tenderizer bottle. Mix vermouth and soy sauce and marinate the steak in the mixture, turning once or twice. Cover with aluminum foil and refrigerate. Turn the steak once again before you go to bed and again in the morning.

Before Serving
Preparation Time: 2 min.   *Cooking Time:* 30 min.

Pour off the marinade. Broil the steak, not too close to the flame, for 15 min. on each side. This will give you medium rare meat. Shorten or lengthen the cooking time if you like your meat either very rare or well done.

Chinese Beef and Peppers

This recipe is offered with a slight apology because, unlike most in this book, it may require you to have your pre-dinner drink in the kitchen. The preparation time immediately before dinner takes only 20 min., but that time involves a fair amount of adding ingredients and stirring.

A cook's greatest asset is a friendly butcher who feels slightly protective about her. If you have that kind, he'll cheerfully slice the sirloin for you. Otherwise, put it in the freezing compartment for an hour before slicing it.

1½ lbs. sirloin, 1 inch thick, sliced in ⅛-inch slivers
4 green peppers, sliced in thin rings

3 medium onions, sliced
5 scallions (green onions) with green tops, sliced
3 to 4 cups boiling water

. . . .

3 tablespoons salad oil
1 teaspoon salt
2 cloves of garlic, chopped
2 teaspoons Accent (monosodium glutamate)
1½ teaspoons sugar

⅛ teaspoon pepper
¾ cup beef bouillon
3 tablespoons cornstarch
2 tablespoons soy sauce
¾ cup cold water

The Night Before

Preparation Time: 15 to 20 min.

Slice the sirloin if the butcher has not already done so and return it to refrigerator.

Pour enough boiling water over pepper rings to cover completely. Let stand 5 min., rinse in cold water. Meanwhile, slice the onions and scallions. Store the onions, scallions and peppers all together in the refrigerator in a covered dish or plastic bag.

Heat oil in a large skillet. Add the peppers, onions, scallions, salt, and garlic. Cook, stirring, over high heat (375° if you're using an electric skillet) for about 3 min. Add beef and cook, stirring, for 3 min. more. Add Accent, sugar, and pepper and cook for 1 more min. Add the bouillon and bring to the boiling point.

While this is cooking, put ¾ cup cold water in a measuring cup and add the cornstarch and soy sauce to it. Mix well, then stir it into the skillet mixture. Stir and cook until the sauce is thickened and translucent—about 4 min.   *Serves 4*

Swedish Meat Balls and Gravy

MEAT BALLS

1 lb. finely ground chuck
2 slices white bread
¼ cup milk
1 small onion, grated
1 egg

1 tablespoon parsley, finely
    chopped
¼ teaspoon ground cloves
¼ teaspoon ground allspice
4 tablespoons (half stick) butter

GRAVY

2 tablespoons flour
1½ cups canned beef broth
¼ to ½ teaspoon soy sauce

1 teaspoon Worcestershire
    sauce
Salt and pepper

The Night Before
Preparation and Cooking Time: 18 min.

Soak bread in milk, then use your hands to mix the two together until the mixture has the consistency of a thick batter. Add meat, onion, egg, parsley, cloves, and allspice, and mix thoroughly. Shape into tiny balls. Melt butter in a large skillet and brown meat balls on all sides. Remove meat balls from skillet with slotted spoon.

Thicken butter remaining in skillet with flour. Slowly add beef broth, Worcestershire sauce, and ¼ teaspoon soy sauce. Cook over low heat, stirring until thickened and smooth. Taste to see if you want to add another ¼ teaspoon soy sauce and/or sal and pepper.

Place m t balls in gravy, cover, and refrigerate.

Before Serving
Cooking Time: 10 min.

Cook, covered, over medium-low heat for 10 min., or until heated through.   *Serves 4*

Stuffed Peppers

Most stuffed pepper recipes involve baking the peppers. Any of these can be adapted to night-before preparation by preparing and stuffing the peppers and refrigerating them at the point where your recipe calls for putting them in the oven. This particular recipe (which we would guess is Hungarian in origin) calls for top-of-the-stove cooking, and we like it best of all.

4 large, firm green peppers
1 lb. chopped chuck
¼ cup uncooked rice
3 onions, 1 grated and 2 sliced
1 egg, slightly beaten

2 teaspoons salt
¼ teaspoon Tabasco
3 tablespoons cold water
3 tablespoons salad oil
1 can (1 lb.) stewed tomatoes

. . . .

¼ cup honey

¼ cup lemon juice

The Night Before
Preparation Time: 15 min.   *Cooking Time:* 1 hr., 15 min.

Put the peppers in a large pot, cover with water and bring to a boil. When water reaches the boiling point, turn off the

13

flame and let the peppers stay in the water for 5 min. Drain and cool. Cut the top inch off, saving the tops. Remove the seeds and membranes and rinse the peppers.

While the peppers are being prepared, grate one onion. Mix together the beef, rice, grated onion, beaten egg, salt, Tabasco, and the 3 tablespoons cold water. Stuff the peppers with the mixture and put them aside.

Heat the salad oil in the pot in which the peppers were scalded. Sauté the 2 sliced onions in the oil until golden, but not crisp. Add the stewed tomatoes and then place the peppers (with their tops put back on) over the sauce. Spoon some of the sauce over the peppers. Cover the pot and simmer over a low flame for 1 hr. Cool and refrigerate.

Before Serving

Preparation Time: 2 min.   *Cooking Time:* 30 min.

Add honey and lemon juice to the sauce and stir well. (You can add a little more salt and some pepper to the sauce at this time if you want to.) Simmer over low flame for 30 min.

Serves 4

☐ LAMB ☐

Lamb Marengo

3 lbs. lamb necks for stewing
½ cup salad oil
2 tablespoons butter
2 onions, chopped
1 teaspoon flour
2 (6 oz.) cans tomato paste

1 clove garlic, crushed or finely
    chopped
1 bay leaf
1 tablespoon salt
4 tablespoons sherry
1 cup water

. . . .

1 lb. small fresh mushrooms, or
1 (6 oz.) can mushrooms

The Night Before

Preparation Time: 20 min.   *Cooking Time:* 1½ hrs.

Heat oil and butter in large skillet. Fry meat briskly until well browned on all sides. Add onions and cook until transparent. Add flour, stirring it in as evenly as possible. Add all other ingredients, *except mushrooms,* and blend well.

Reduce heat, cover, and cook gently for 1½ hours. Remove from heat, allow to cool, and refrigerate, covered.

Before Serving

Preparation Time: 5 min.   *Cooking Time:* 30 min.

Wipe mushrooms with damp cloth, or rinse in cold water. If canned mushrooms are used, drain them and set aside.

Over low heat, cook the meat and sauce for 15 min., stirring occasionally. Add mushrooms and cook for 15 min. longer.

Serves 4

Curried Meat Balls

MEAT BALLS

1½ lbs. ground lamb—some supermarkets sell this as "lamb patties"

2 cloves garlic, minced

1 egg

½ cup pignolia (pine nuts)

⅓ cup finely chopped parsley

¾ teaspoon salt

4 tablespoons olive oil

CURRY SAUCE

6 tablespoons butter or margarine

2 stalks celery, diced

1 large apple, cored and diced (unpeeled)

1 large onion, diced

2 to 3 teaspoons curry powder

2 cups tomato juice

¼ cup tomato paste

. . . .

Scant tablespoonful chutney

The Night Before
Preparation and Cooking Time: 25 min.

Combine lamb, garlic, egg, nuts, parsley, and salt and mix thoroughly. Then add 4 tablespoons of the olive oil and mix again. Heat remaining 2 tablespoons olive oil in very large skillet. Brown meat balls for 8 to 10 min.—they should be well browned on the outside but medium rare in the center.

While meat balls are browning, prepare curry sauce. Melt the butter in a 2-quart pot—one that also can be used as a serving dish. Add the diced celery, apple, and onion. Cook over low heat until celery softens and onion becomes translucent. Stir in curry powder, starting with 2 teaspoons and increasing according to taste; cook very gently for 5 min. longer. Add tomato juice and cook over medium heat for 5 min. Stir in tomato paste to thicken sauce.

Add meat balls to sauce, cover, and refrigerate.

Preparation Time: 1 min.   *Cooking Time:* 15 min.

Cook, covered, on top of stove over medium-low heat until heated through—about 15 min. Remove from heat and stir in chutney. Serve over boiled white rice.   *Serves 4*

Lamb Shishkebab

2 lbs. boned leg of lamb, cut   ½ cup lemon juice
    in cubes   ½ cup lime juice
1 #2 can boiled onions   ½ cup olive oil
1 green pepper, cut in cubes   1½ teaspoons salt

The Night Before
Preparation Time: 12 min.

Thread the lamb cubes, onions, and green pepper alternately on four long skewers. Lay skewers flat in a large roasting pan.

Combine all other ingredients and mix well. Pour over the filled skewers. Cover pan with foil and refrigerate. Turn skewers once, several hours later or the next morning.

Before Serving
Preparation Time: 3 min.   *Cooking Time:* 20 to 30 min.

Broil the filled skewers about 4 in. from heat for 10 to 15 min., depending on how well done you like your meat. Turn and brush with marinade again and broil for another 10 to 15 min.   *Serves 4*

Kafta

1½ lbs. ground lamb   3 heaping tablespoons pignolia
1 medium onion, chopped fine   (pine nuts)
2 cups parsley, chopped fine   1¼ teaspoons salt
2 tablespoons butter   ⅛ teaspoon pepper

· · · · · · · · · · · · · · ·

1 can (1 lb.) stewed tomatoes

Mix the lamb, onion, parsley, pignolia, salt, and pepper lightly but thoroughly. Your hands will do this job better than any utensil. Divide the meat into 8 cakes, no more than ¾ inch thick. Sauté in butter over a low flame (300° in an electric skillet) for 10 to 12 minutes. Arrange the meat cakes in a shallow oven dish. Cover and refrigerate.

Before Serving

Preparation Time: 2 min.   *Cooking Time:* 30 min.

Pour the stewed tomatoes over the meat cakes. Bake (uncovered) at 325° for 30 min.

Serves 4

Lamb Stew with Dumplings

2 lbs. lean shoulder of lamb, cut in 2-inch cubes
1 large onion, sliced
¼ cup salad oil
1½ teaspoons salt
1 teaspoon paprika

¼ teaspoon basil
1 garlic clove, chopped
6 carrots, cut in 1-inch cubes
1 can (8 oz.) small boiled onions

. . . .

1 can (1 lb.) small white potatoes
1 can (13½ oz.) beef bouillon

1 cup Bisquick
3 oz. milk
1 teaspoon parsley flakes

The Night Before

Preparation and Cooking Time: 20 min.

Heat the salad oil in a large skillet. Cook the sliced onion until slightly soft. Add the lamb cubes and brown on all sides. With a slotted spoon, remove the onion and the lamb from the skillet and transfer to a large stove-to-table casserole. Add the salt, paprika, basil, garlic, carrots, and boiled onions to the casserole and mix gently. Cover and refrigerate.

Preparation Time: 6 min.   *Cooking Time:* 1 hr.

Add the drained potatoes and the beef bouillon to the casserole. Stir. Cover and simmer over medium flame. Mix Bisquick, milk, and parsley flakes with a fork. When the stew has simmered for 40 min., top the bubbling stew with spoonfuls of the dumpling mixture. Cook, uncovered, for 10 min.; then cover and cook for 10 min. more.   *Serves 4*

Moussaka

1½ lbs. ground lamb	2 cloves garlic, chopped
2 medium eggplants, pared and sliced	1 can (1 lb.) tomatoes
	1 can tomato paste
¼ cup olive oil	2 teaspoons oregano
¼ cup flour	1 tablespoon parsley, chopped
2 medium onions, diced	1½ teaspoons salt

. . . .

¾ cup ricotta cheese (optional)

The Night Before

Preparation Time: 35 min.   *Cooking Time:* 15 min.
(in addition to cooking during preparation time)

Peel and slice eggplant into half-inch slices. Heat olive oil in a large skillet. Dust the eggplant slices lightly with flour and sauté in oil for about 5 min. on each side. Remove eggplant from skillet and set aside. Place diced onion and garlic in the skillet and cook, stirring, until onion is transparent. Add ground lamb and brown it, stirring frequently. Add tomatoes, tomato paste, oregano, parsley, and salt. Stir. Let the mixture simmer for 15 min.

Place a layer of eggplant in a casserole. Top with a layer of meat sauce. Alternate layers until all ingredients are used, ending with a layer of meat sauce. Cover and refrigerate.

Preparation Time: 2 min.   *Cooking Time:* 1 hr.

Heat oven to 350°. If desired, top moussaka with spoonfuls of ricotta. Bake, uncovered, for 1 hr.   *Serves 4 to 5*

Skillet Lamb Chop Dinner

Shoulder lamb chops (1 or 2   Canned peach halves (2 per
   per person)   person)
Soy sauce   Jelly
Water

The Night Before

Preparation Time: 5 min.

Mix soy sauce and water in equal parts, making enough for marinating the number of chops you are using. Lay the chops in a large shallow pan (preferably not aluminum) and pour soy sauce mixture over them. Turn chops to coat well. Cover with waxed paper or aluminum foil and refrigerate.

Drain peaches. If you're cooking in large quantities and won't be able to fit the peaches into the skillet with the chops, arrange them in a pan that can go directly under the broiler. If you'll be able to fit the peaches into the skillet, place them on a large plate. Put half a teaspoon of jelly into the center of each peach. Cover and refrigerate. Turn chops once the next morning.

Before Serving

Preparation Time: 3 min.   *Cooking Time:* 20 min.

Pour off sauce. Cook chops for 10 min. on each side in a large, ungreased skillet. (Set the control at 375° if using an electric pan.) If you have room, tuck the peaches in the skillet for the last 5 min. of cooking. If you don't have enough room, pop the peaches under the broiler for 5 min.

Kusa Mihshi: Stuffed Squash in the Lebanese Manner

(This same recipe can be used for stuffing eggplant; substitute 2 medium eggplants for the 6 squash.)

6 yellow crookneck squash
½ lb. ground lamb or beef
1 cup raw white rice
½ cup (1 stick) butter, melted
1 teaspoon salt

¼ teaspoon pepper
1 teaspoon cinnamon
1 can (1 lb.) tomatoes or tomato purée, mixed with 1 can water

The Night Before

Preparation Time: 13 min.   *Cooking Time:* 45 min.

Cut off the "necks" of the squash. (Don't discard them—you can cook and serve them as plain old squash.) Scoop the squash and seeds from the rounded parts, leaving as thin a shell as possible—a melon ball cutter does this nicely. (The scooped-out squash may *also* be cooked as plain old squash.)

Combine meat, rice, melted butter, salt, pepper, and cinnamon. Mix thoroughly. Spoon filling lightly—don't pack it down—into squash shells. The shells should be only two thirds full. Place in a deep, heavy pot. Mix tomato purée or tomatoes and water. Pour into and over stuffed squash. Cover and simmer gently for 45 min. Refrigerate.

Before Serving

Preparation Time: 1 min.   *Cooking Time:* 15 min.

Place pot, still covered, on top of stove and simmer gently for 15 min. Baste squash once or twice with sauce in pot.

Serves 3 to 4 as a main course

☐ VEAL ☐

Lake Mohegan Veal Chops

6–8 veal chops, each ¾ inch
    thick
5 cloves garlic
⅔ cup salad oil

4 tablespoons ketchup
2 tablespoons vinegar
½ teaspoon pepper
⅓ cup soy sauce

The Night Before
Preparation Time: 5 to 10 min.

Place all ingredients other than veal chops in a blender and
blend for 20 seconds. If you have no blender, crush the garlic
cloves and mix them with the other ingredients by hand. Place
the blended mixture in a shallow baking pan. Put the chops
in the mixture, turning a couple of times to coat well. Cover
the pan with aluminum foil and place in refrigerator. Turn
the chops over once after a few hours or the next morning.

Before Serving
Preparation Time: 5 min.   *Cooking Time:* 20 to 25 min.

Remove chops from sauce. You have a choice of cooking
method. Our personal order of preference is as follows:

Grill over charcoal for 15 to 20 min., turning once.

or

Heat electric frying pan to 350°. Cook chops for 20 min.,
    turning once.

or

Put chops in broiler and broil for 15 min., turning once.

or

Cook over medium-high heat in an ungreased skillet for
    about 10 min. on each side.
    (This method is fourth on the list because it's hard to cook
    more than a few chops at a time in a nonelectric skillet

and you may have to juggle two skillets if you're feeding more than two people. A large electric skillet can take all the chops at once.) *Serves 4*

Veal Paprikash and Noodles

2 lbs. veal shoulder, cut in 1-inch cubes
2 teaspoons salt
2 tablespoons flour
2 tablespoons paprika
2 tablespoons salad oil

1 clove garlic, minced
2 lbs. canned tomatoes
2 teaspoons sugar
1 bay leaf
8 oz. package noodles
1 tablespoon butter

. . . .

½ teaspoon caraway seeds

1 cup sour cream

The Night Before

Preparation Time: 30 min.   *Cooking Time:* 35 to 40 min.

Heat the oil in a 4-quart casserole, add the garlic, and cook for about 5 min. over low heat. Meanwhile, put flour, salt, and paprika into a paper bag and shake the veal cubes in this mixture until well coated. Brown the meat in the oil on all sides, using moderate heat. When well browned, add to the veal cubes the tomatoes, sugar, and bay leaf. Cover and simmer until veal is tender—about 35 min.

While the veal is browning, cook noodles according to package directions. Melt butter. Drain noodles and toss with butter. Set aside.

When veal is done, place noodles on top of meat in casserole. (Do *not* mix the noodles with the sauce.) Cover the casserole and refrigerate.

Before Serving

Preparation Time: 5 min.   *Cooking Time:* 1 hr., 5 min.

Place covered casserole in a cold oven, still leaving the noodles on top of meat. Set oven for 400° and bake for 1 hr.

Stir in caraway seeds and sour cream, and *now* the noodles may be mixed with the rest of the casserole. Bake, uncovered, just until the sour cream heats through—about 5 min.

Serves 5 to 6

Veal Marinara

1 cup canned Italian tomatoes	1 tablespoon chopped parsley
½ cup olive oil	¼ teaspoon salt
2 cloves garlic	Dash of pepper
1 teaspoon oregano	

• • • • • • • • • • • •

2 lbs. veal cutlet, cut ¼ inch thick	Salt
3 tablespoons butter	Pepper

The Night Before

Preparation Time: 5 min.   *Cooking Time:* 30 min.

Put all the ingredients in the blender. Run it very briefly—about 15 seconds. (If you have no blender, put the tomatoes through a sieve and crush the garlic before mixing with the other ingredients.) Pour sauce into a saucepan. Cover and simmer gently for half an hour, stirring occasionally. Cool slightly and refrigerate.

Before Serving

Preparation Time: 5 min.   *Cooking Time:* 16 min.

Melt butter in a large skillet (set at 275° if you're using an electric pan). Sprinkle the veal with a little salt and very little pepper. Sauté for about 3 min. on each side. While the veal is being sautéed, warm the sauce slightly. Pour the sauce over the veal and reduce the heat a bit (to 200° if using an electric pan). Cover and cook for 10 min., turning veal once after about 5 min.

Serves 4

Italian Veal with Tuna Sauce

This dish is tailor-made for the night-before cook. In fact, it can't be made by any other kind. The veal *must* be cooked the night before, refrigerated overnight, and served cold. True gourmets insist that it should be served with cold rice. If your crew balks at that notion, go ahead and use hot rice or buttered noodles. We won't tell on you!

Just one hint: If you're going to double or treble the recipe to use it for company, have your butcher make a separate roll of each 2 lbs. of veal. If you have more than 2 lbs. in a single roll, it's going to throw the cooking time off considerably.

2 lbs. boneless leg of veal, rolled and tied	1 tablespoon salt
	¼ teaspoon pepper
1 small can (3 oz.) tuna fish	¼ cup olive oil
6 or 7 rolled anchovy filets, quartered	3 tablespoons lemon juice
	3 tablespoons chopped sour pickle
1 small onion, chopped	
1½ cups dry white wine	

The Night Before

Preparation Time: 12 min.   *Cooking Time:* 1¾ hrs.

Place the meat in a heavy saucepan with the onion, anchovies, tuna, wine, salt, and pepper. Cover and simmer over low flame for 1¾ hrs.

Remove the meat to a casserole. Blend the sauce in an electric blender. (If you don't have one, put the sauce through a fine sieve twice.) Then stir in the olive oil, lemon juice, and chopped pickle. Pour the sauce over the meat. Cover the casserole and refrigerate it.

Before Serving

Preparation Time: 5 min.

Remove the meat from the sauce and slice thinly. The sauce can be served directly from the casserole in which it was stored.   *Serves 5 to 6*

Veal Scallops Louise

8 thin veal scallops (1½ to 1¾ lbs.)
4 tablespoons lemon juice
Salt and pepper

4 tablespoons (½ stick) butter
½ pint (1 cup) sour cream
5 to 6 oz. grated Swiss cheese

The Night Before
Preparation and Cooking Time: 12 min.

Salt and pepper veal, sprinkle with lemon juice, and let stand for 10 min. Pour off lemon juice into small saucepan and reserve. Heat butter in large skillet and sauté veal briefly on each side—just until it turns white. (This will take only 2 or 3 min.) Place veal scallops on broiler pan or in shallow baking dish. Spread sour cream over each scallop and top with grated cheese. Cover with waxed paper or foil and refrigerate. Add any butter left in the skillet to lemon juice in saucepan. Cover saucepan and refrigerate.

Before Serving
Preparation Time: 1 min.   *Cooking Time: 5 to 8 min.*

Preheat broiler. Broil veal until cheese browns. While it is broiling, heat lemon and butter mixture in saucepan over low flame on top of stove. Remove veal from broiler, pour sauce over it, and serve.

Serves 4

Veau Chaud

Although breast of veal is an inexpensive cut of meat, it lends itself to interesting treatment and dramatic presentation. This "hot veal" is served cold—"hot" refers to the sausage stuffing and the anchovy-olive dressing. It's perfect for a summer menu, or for the buffet table.

3½ lbs. breast of veal, with deep pocket for stuffing
1 tablespoon salad oil
1 lb. Italian sweet sausage
1 small onion, finely chopped
1 cup cooked rice (the quick cooking kind)
2 tablespoons chopped parsley
1 clove garlic, crushed
1 egg

ANCHOVY-OLIVE DRESSING

1 cup mayonnaise
6 anchovies
8 stuffed green olives
1 clove garlic
2 slices onion

The Night Before

Preparation Time: 30 min.   *Cooking Time:* 1½ hrs.

While the rice is cooking, remove sausage meat from casings. Combine with rice, onion, parsley, garlic, and egg. Pack this mixture into the pocket of the breast of veal. Close the opening with skewers or toothpicks. Use paper towels to wipe surface of veal dry.

Preheat oven to 325°. Heat oil in a large skillet (preferably one that can go from top of stove to oven). Brown veal on all sides. Remove from heat. Wrap in aluminum foil and bake for 1½ hours.

While the veal is browning, prepare the dressing. Put all ingredients into the container of an electric blender and blend until anchovies and olives are chopped. If you are not using a blender, mince the anchovies and onions, crush the garlic, chop the olives, and stir all into the mayonnaise.

Refrigerate veal and dressing in separate covered serving dishes.

Before Serving

Preparation Time: 4 min.

Slice veal. Serve sauce separately.   *Serves 4 to 5*

Veal Cordon Bleu

(Allow either 1 or 2 veal scallops per person, depending on the size of the scallops you buy and the voracity of the crew you feed.)

Large, thin veal scallops	Flavored bread crumbs
1 slice of prosciutto ham for each scallop	1 egg, mixed with ½ cup milk, for each 5 or 6 scallops
1 slice of cheese (mozzarella, Cheddar, or American are all good) for each scallop	

. . . .

Salad oil for frying

The Night Before
Preparation Time: 15 to 20 min.

On half of each veal scallop, place 1 slice of ham and 1 slice of cheese. Fold scallop over, covering filling completely. Seal edges with toothpicks. Coat each scallop in the bread crumbs, then dip into the egg-milk mixture, and then in the bread crumbs again. Store in refrigerator, putting sheets of waxed paper between layers of veal scallops. (One of the advantages of making this dish in two steps is that all breaded foods tend to keep their breading intact during the cooking process if they've been refrigerated before cooking.)

Before Serving
Preparation Time: 5 min.　　　　　*Cooking Time:* 10 to 15 min.

Heat salad oil and fry scallops until golden brown—about 10 to 15 min., turning once.

Veal Soubise

The outstanding feature of this veal roast is its beautiful texture, achieved by cooking it in a covered pot, rather than an open roasting pan. An electric skillet is perfect for this recipe; it provides accurate, even heat and also makes this a one-pot operation. You may, of course, use instead a deep, heavy pot and your trusty old stove burners. As you must know by now, we are appliance addicts and prefer the electric skillet.

3 lbs. boneless veal roast, rolled and tied	Small bay leaf, or ½ large bay leaf
2 tablespoons salad oil	2 tablespoons parsley
2 tablespoons butter or margarine	¼ teaspoon thyme
	¼ teaspoon salt
2 large onions, sliced	¼ teaspoon black pepper

The Night Before

Preparation Time: 20 min.   *Cooking Time:* 1½ hrs.

Heat butter and oil in skillet and brown veal on all sides—takes about 12 min. Remove veal, lower heat, and add onions, bay leaf, parsley, and thyme to skillet. Cover and cook just until onions are softened and gold-colored. Rub browned veal with salt and pepper and place in skillet (or in pot on top of stove). Set electric skillet heat control to "simmer," or simmer on top of stove over medium low flame, and cook for 1½ hrs. Remove from heat. Discard bay leaf.

Pour sauce—including the onions—into the container of an electric blender and blend until sauce is smooth. If you do not have a blender, mash onions through a sieve and stir into the sauce. Return veal and sauce to pan, cover, and refrigerate.

Before Serving

Preparation Time: 5 min.   *Cooking Time:* 20 min.

Heat both veal and sauce slowly for 20 min. Slice veal, pour sauce into gravy boat, and serve.   *Serves 6*

Creole Veal Scallops

8 veal scallops
1 egg, lightly beaten
¼ cup milk
1½ cups bread crumbs
¼ cup salad oil
1 onion, coarsely chopped

1 cup (about 3 large stalks) diced celery
1 green pepper, chopped
1 large can (2 lbs.) tomatoes
1 teaspoon salt

The Night Before

Preparation Time: 15 min.   *Cooking Time:* 1 hr., 15 min.

Mix egg with milk. Spread bread crumbs on a flat surface. Dip veal in bread crumbs, then in egg mixture, then once again in bread crumbs. Heat oil in large skillet (325° in electric skillet) or Dutch oven and brown veal scallops on both sides. When brown, add all other ingredients, lower heat, cover, and simmer for 1 hr., 15 min. Refrigerate.

Before Serving

Cooking Time: 15 to 20 min.

Place covered pot over medium-low heat, or set electric skillet at 250°, and cook for 15 or 20 min., until heated through.

Serves 4

☐ PORK ☐

Apricot Pork Chops

8 pork chops
1 tablespoon olive oil
Salt
Pepper
2 tablespoons wine vinegar

1 large can (1 lb., 14 oz.) pitted
  apricot halves
2 tablespoons pine nuts or slivered almonds

The Night Before
Preparation and Cooking Time: 12 min.

Heat the olive oil in a large skillet (or two skillets if the chops won't all fit in one), setting the skillet at 325° if you're using an electric one. Brown the chops for 4 to 5 min. on each side.

While the chops are browning, mix the apricot halves and their juice, the vinegar, and the nuts.

When the chops have browned, sprinkle them lightly with salt and pepper. Place them in a shallow oven-to-table roasting pan and pour the fruit sauce over the chops. Cover and refrigerate.

Before Serving
Preparation Time: 1 min.   *Cooking Time: 45 min.*

Heat oven to 350°. Bake chops, covered, for 30 min. Uncover and bake for 15 min. longer.   *Serves 4*

Burgundy Pork Chops

8 lean pork chops
¼ cup flour
1 teaspoon salt
2 tablespoons salad oil
2 tablespoons prepared mustard

1 tablespoon brown sugar
1 tablespoon cornstarch
1 cup Burgundy
1 cup crushed pineapple

31

Mix flour and salt in a paper bag. Drop pork chops in and shake vigorously until chops are coated with flour. Heat fat and brown chops until light brown. Place the chops in a casserole and place covered casserole in refrigerator.

While the chops are browning, blend the mustard, sugar, and cornstarch in a small saucepan. Add the wine and pineapple and cook, stirring until it reaches the boiling point. Cool slightly and store, in the covered saucepan, in the refrigerator.

Before Serving

Preparation Time: 2 min.   *Cooking Time:* 1 hr.

Heat oven to 350°. Heat saucepan of sauce. When hot, pour over the pork chops and place the pork chop casserole, uncovered, in the oven for 1 hr.   *Serves 4*

Barbecued Pork Chops

This dish combines well with the Zucchini Casserole on page 107, since both require the same baking temperature and time.

8 pork chops	1 teaspoon salt
1½ tablespoons dry mustard	¼ teaspoon pepper
1 tablespoon Worcestershire sauce	1½ cups ketchup
2 cloves garlic, crushed	3 tablespoons olive oil

The Night Before
Preparation and Cooking Time: 12 min.

Heat 1 tablespoon olive oil in a large skillet (325° if you're using an electric skillet). If you have more chops than will fit into your skillet comfortably, you will either have to use two skillets simultaneously or brown the chops in two shifts, increasing your in-kitchen time slightly. Brown chops for 4 to 5 min. on each side.

While the chops are browning, make a paste of the mustard and Worcestershire sauce; mix with all the other ingredients, including the remaining 2 tablespoons olive oil. Remove chops from the skillet and place in a shallow oven-to-table roasting pan or wide casserole. Pour sauce over chops. Cover and refrigerate.

Before Serving

Preparation Time: 1 min.   *Cooking Time:* 45 min.

Heat oven to 350°. Bake chops, covered, for 30 min. Uncover and bake for 15 min. longer.   *Serves 4*

Sweet and Pungent Spareribs

3½ to 4 lbs. spareribs
2 teaspoons salad oil
½ teaspoon salt
1 clove garlic
1 green pepper, cut in 1-inch chunks
1 can (13 oz.) pineapple chunks

1½ tablespoons cornstarch
3 tablespoons sugar
¾ cup cold water
6 tablespoons red wine vinegar
1 teaspoon soy sauce
¼ cup maraschino cherries

The Night Before

Preparation Time: 25 min.   *Cooking Time:* 1¼ hrs.
                                               (including preparation time)

Cut meat into serving pieces (or, better still, have the butcher do it for you). Heat oven to 325°. Place meat on rack in uncovered roasting pan and bake for 1¼ hrs. Remove meat to a plate. Remove rack and drain all fat out of the pan. Replace meat in pan without rack. Cool slightly, cover with foil and refrigerate.

While the spareribs are baking, prepare sauce as follows: Heat the oil in a saucepan. Add the peeled clove of garlic and the salt and cook slowly for 10 min. Meanwhile, cut the peppers into chunks. Remove the garlic and discard it. Add to the heated oil all the syrup from the can of pineapple and the green pepper. Cook for 10 min. Meanwhile, blend the water with the cornstarch, sugar, vinegar, and soy sauce. Add this mixture to the sauce. Cook, stirring frequently, for about 5 min., until the sauce is thickened and translucent.

Add the pineapple chunks and cherries. Remove from stove, cool slightly, and store in the covered saucepan in the refrigerator.

Before Serving

Preparation Time: 5 min.   *Cooking Time:* 25 min.

Heat oven to 325° and place pan containing spareribs in oven. Bake for 5 min. During this time, reheat the sauce, stirring occasionally. When ribs have baked for 5 min., pour sauce over ribs and bake 20 min. longer.

This is excellent served with hot rice.   *Serves 4*

Sausage in French Roll Crust

¾ lb. sausage meat   ⅓ cup water
¼ lb. ground round steak   1 egg
1 medium onion, chopped   2 teaspoons mustard
2 tablespoons butter   2 brown-and-serve French rolls
½ teaspoon salt   (about 8 inches long)
½ teaspoon marjoram

. . . .

2 additional tablespoons butter   1 clove garlic, crushed

The Night Before

Preparation Time: 25 min.

Sauté chopped onion in 2 tablespoons butter. Add sausage meat and cook gently for 5 to 10 min., mashing it with a fork as it cooks.

Add ground round steak and cook until browned.

Cut the ends from the brown and serve rolls. Gently hollow out the rolls, leaving the thinnest possible shell, and break the bread into soft crumbs. Add crumbs to the meat mixture. Add the egg, salt, marjoram, mustard, and water. Cover and refrigerate in the pan in which it was cooked. Refrigerate shells of French rolls.

Before Serving

Preparation Time: 10 min.   *Cooking Time:* 10 to 12 min.

Heat oven to 400°. While oven is heating, melt 2 tablespoons butter and add crushed garlic. Simmer gently for 2 min., remove from flame and set aside. Briefly reheat meat mixture over medium flame. Stuff French roll shells with meat mixture, brush with melted butter and bake for 10 to 12 min., until crusts are lightly browned. Slice and serve.   *Serves 4*

Real Fine Hambake

This is a nice touch for the ready-to-eat ham steaks or smoked ham slices you buy in the supermarket, or for just plain old leftover ham.

2 lbs. smoked or cooked ham
    steaks or slices (¼ inch
    thick)
2 tablespoons butter
2 tablespoons salad oil
2 onions, diced

2 green peppers, diced
2 cloves garlic, crushed
1 large can (3 cups) tomatoes,
    with their liquid
¼ teaspoon oregano

The Night Before
Preparation and Cooking Time: 25 min.

Heat butter and oil in a large skillet. Brown ham slices lightly, remove from skillet, and place side by side in a baking dish. Set aside.

Add the chopped onions to the fat remaining in the skillet, cover, and cook over low heat for 4 or 5 min. Add the sliced peppers and crushed garlic, cover, and cook over very low heat for another 5 or 6 min. Add the tomatoes and liquid and the oregano. Boil rapidly (uncovered) until most of the liquid has boiled down.

Spread the onion-pepper-tomato mixture over the ham slices. Cover and refrigerate.

Before Serving

Preparation Time: ½ min.   Cooking Time: 20 min.

Bake, uncovered, in a 350° oven for 20 min.   *Serves 4*

Cranberry Ham Slice

¾ cup granulated sugar
¾ cup brown sugar
1½ tablespoons dry mustard
½ cup cider vinegar

4 tablespoons butter
1 small (8 oz.) can whole cranberry sauce

. . . .

Pre-cooked ham slice, 1 inch thick (about 2 lbs.)

The Night Before

Preparation Time: 5 min.   Cooking Time: 10 min.

Mix the granulated and brown sugar and mustard in a small saucepan. Add vinegar and butter and stir. Simmer for 8 min., stirring occasionally. Add cranberry sauce and continue cooking for 2 min., stirring 3 or 4 times. Let mixture cool. Cover and refrigerate.

Before Serving

Preparation Time: 2 min.   Cooking Time: 15 min.

While your oven is heating to 350°, place the pan of sauce on the stove to warm slightly. Place the ham slice in a baking dish and pour sauce over it. Bake, uncovered, for 15 min.

Serves 4

Tropikabobs

2 to 2½ lbs. "ready-to-eat" (smoked or pre-cooked) ham, cut in 1½-inch cubes
1 can (11 to 12 oz.) mandarin oranges
1 can (13½ oz.) pineapple chunks
¼ cup pineapple juice from canned pineapple chunks
2 tablespoons lemon juice
8 tablespoons (1 stick) butter, or 4 tablespoons butter and 4 tablespoons margarine
3 tablespoons light brown sugar
¼ teaspoon dry mustard
2 whole cloves

The Night Before
Preparation and Cooking Time: 13 min.

Drain pineapple and oranges, reserving ¼ cup pineapple juice.

Melt butter in small, heavy saucepan. Add lemon juice, pineapple juice, sugar, mustard, and cloves. Cook together gently for 3 min. Cover saucepan and refrigerate.

Thread ham cubes, pineapple chunks, and orange sections alternately on 4 or 5 twelve-inch skewers. Leave last half inch of each skewer unfilled. Suspend the skewers across the top of a shallow baking dish. If you haven't used all the pineapple chunks or orange sections, place the rest in the bottom of the baking dish. Cover with foil or plastic wrap and refrigerate.

Before Serving
Preparation Time: 4 min.   *Cooking Time: 8 to 10 min.*

Preheat broiler. Heat sauce, which will have solidified while in the refrigerator, until it melts—this will take only a minute or two. Put baking dish, with filled skewers suspended across the top, on bottom level of broiler. Baste with half of sauce.

Broil 4 to 5 min. Turn, baste with rest of sauce, and broil for 4 to 5 min. longer.

Place skewers on serving platter and spoon sauce that has dripped into the baking dish over them. Its's nice, incidentally, if the serving platter has a bed of boiled white rice on it.

□ FISH AND SHELLFISH □

Spicy Shrimp Dinner

This recipe reflects one of our deep-seated prejudices. We hate to start a shrimp dish with raw, unshelled shrimp. We just don't have the patience for the monumental job of shelling dozens of shrimp and removing those loathsome, evasive little black spines. We prefer to buy our shrimp already cleaned. In some stores you can buy it cleaned but uncooked; in others you must take it cooked if you want to avoid the cleaning job. We'll settle for either. This is a more expensive way of buying shrimp, but the price differential is not as great as it appears at first blush. Remember that when you buy raw unshelled shrimp, you're paying for a lot of shells that will end up in your garbage pail. In any event, if you were a prize biology student and like the spine dissecting job, buy your shrimp in the raw and cook them the night before. (Plunge shrimp into boiling water, lower heat, and simmer for 7 min.) Our preparation time is based on the assumption that you are starting off with cleaned, cooked shrimp.

4 slices bacon
3 tablespoons olive oil
1 large onion, finely chopped
½ cup celery, diced
1 clove garlic, chopped
1 tablespoon flour
1 green pepper, diced
1 can (1 lb.) tomatoes
¼ cup tomato juice
¼ cup finely chopped parsley

1 tablespoon vinegar
1 tablespoon sugar
2 tablespoons chili powder
¼ teaspoon thyme
1 teaspoon Worcestershire
    sauce
1 teaspoon horseradish
1 tablespoon lemon juice
½ teaspoon dry mustard

. . . .

1½ lbs. cooked, cleaned shrimp
    (buy 2¾ lbs. if you're buy-
    ing them with shells)

1 can (1 lb.) okra or peas
1 can (3 oz.) whole mushrooms

The Night Before

Preparation Time: 20 min.   **Cooking Time:** 35 min.

Chop the onion, garlic, and celery. Cook the bacon until crisp, but do not discard bacon fat during the cooking process. Remove the bacon from the pan and set it aside. Add the olive oil to the bacon fat and cook the onion, celery, and garlic in the combined fats for about 5 min., until the onion is transparent. Add the flour, stir, and remove the pan from the stove. Add the crumbled bacon and all the other ingredients (except the shrimp, okra or peas, and mushrooms). Stir well and simmer over a low flame for 35 min., stirring occasionally. Cool slightly, cover, and refrigerate.

Before Serving

Preparation Time: 2 min.   **Cooking Time:** 30 min.

Add the shrimp, okra or peas, and mushrooms to the sauce and cook over a low flame for 30 min. This is excellent served with boiled rice.   *Serves 6*

Sweet and Sour Shrimp

The preparation and cooking time for this dish is a combined half hour. You will have to stay in or near the kitchen for most of that time to stir or to add ingredients. You won't be kept busy much of the time, however, and you'll have ample opportunity to prepare a molded salad or a vegetable in between working on the shrimp sauce. We like a gelatin salad and rice with this dish.

1 tablespoon salad oil
½ teaspoon salt
3 carrots, cut in thin diagonal slices
2 green peppers, cut in cubes
1 can (13½ oz.) pineapple chunks

1 clove garlic
2 tablespoons cornstarch
1½ teaspoons soy sauce
2 tablespoons sugar
⅓ cup red wine vinegar
1¼ cups water

. . . .

1 lb. cooked, cleaned shrimp (Buy 1¾ lbs. if you buy your shrimp in the shell. See note on page 51.)

The Night Before
Preparation and Cooking Time: 30 min.

Heat the salad oil in a stove-to-table casserole. Add the salt and the peeled clove of garlic and simmer slowly for 5 min., stirring occasionally. Meanwhile, pare and slice the carrots and wash and dice the green peppers. When the garlic has cooked for 5 min., remove it and add to the oil the liquid from the can of pineapple and the carrots. Cook for 5 min., stirring occasionally. Then add the green peppers. Simmer for 10 min. Meanwhile, combine the cornstarch, soy sauce, sugar, and red wine vinegar. When the sauce has cooked for 10 min. after the addition of the green peppers, add the cornstarch mixture slowly, stirring well. Add the water and continue cooking, stirring, until sauce is thick—about 2 to 3 min. Remove from stove, add pineapple chunks, cool, cover, and refrigerate.

Before Serving
Preparation Time: 3 min.   *Cooking Time: 10 min.*

Add the shrimp to the sauce and simmer over a low flame for about 10 min., until mixture is warmed through. You have to watch the heat at this point, so that the sauce doesn't scorch. You can save yourself some watching and stirring time if you warm the casserole with an insulating pad over your burner.   *Serves 4*

Lobster Tails Fra Diavolo

8 lobster tails (We use frozen lobster tails, which tend to be small, and we find 2 per portion are needed. If the lobster tails you buy are large, 1 per person may be enough. If you are using frozen lobster, be sure it is thawed before you start your night-before preparation.)

¼ cup olive oil
1 clove garlic, chopped
1 can (1 lb.) plum tomatoes
¼ teaspoon crushed red pepper seeds
1¼ teaspoons oregano
½ teaspoon salt
Dash pepper

The Night Before

Preparation Time: 15 min.   Cooking Time: 12 min.

Heat the olive oil in a saucepan and cook the chopped garlic in the oil over a low flame for about 2 min. Add all the other ingredients except the lobster. Stir; simmer for 10 min., stirring occasionally.

While the sauce is simmering, cut through the soft cartilage of each lobster tail with a kitchen scissors and bend the edges back to expose a maximum amount of the lobster meat. Arrange the lobster tails in the baking dish in which they will be cooked. Cover the dish with aluminum foil and refrigerate.

When the sauce has cooked for 10 min., allow it to cool slightly, then cover and refrigerate it.

Before Serving

Preparation Time: 3 min.   Cooking Time: 25 min.

Heat oven to 350°. While it is heating, place the pan of sauce on the stove and reheat slightly. Pour the sauce over the lobster tails and bake for 25 min.   *Serves 4*

Crabmeat Casserole

2 cans crabmeat (8 oz. each)	2 beaten egg yolks
6 tablespoons butter	2 tablespoons sherry
6 tablespoons flour	1 cup soft bread crumbs
3 cups milk	1 tablespoon minced parsley
⅛ teaspoon pepper	1 teaspoon minced onion
½ teaspoon celery salt	

. . . .

¼ cup fine, dry bread crumbs	1 tablespoon butter
Paprika	

The Night Before

Preparation Time: 30 min.   *Cooking Time:* 10 min.

Melt the 6 tablespoons butter. Add flour and blend. Add milk, celery salt, and pepper. Cook over low heat, stirring constantly until thickened. Add egg yolks and cook 2 min. longer, stirring constantly.

Remove from stove and add sherry, soft bread crumbs, crabmeat, parsley, and onion. Mix gently and pour into greased 1½ quart casserole. Refrigerate.

Before Serving

Preparation Time: 5 min.   *Cooking Time:* 40 min.

Heat oven to 400°. Sprinkle dry bread crumbs over casserole and dot with butter. Sprinkle lightly with paprika.

Bake, uncovered, for 40 min.   *Serves 4*

Shellfish à la Tomorrow: "Eat, Drink, and Be Merry, for Tomorrow We Diet"

We have given this creation its peculiar name because we haven't the courage to use its real name: fried cream, or, in French, *crèmes frites*. (Actually, it's a kind of seafood croquette.) In this day and age, when even dog food has public relations experts slaving over it, you've got to watch your images—and fried cream sounds more fattening than anything we can imagine. We trust that fried cream by any other name . . .

1⅔ cups of any one or any combination of canned or cooked shellfish:	½ teaspoon oregano
	Scant 3 tablespoons flour
	1⅓ cups very hot milk
Crabmeat, flaked	Dash black pepper
Lobster, flaked or finely diced	1 egg yolk
	⅓ cup heavy cream
Shrimp, finely diced	⅓ cup grated Swiss cheese
Clams, minced	3 eggs, lightly beaten
2½ tablespoons butter	2 tablespoons salad oil
2 scallions, minced	1 cup flour
4 tablespoons sherry	3 cups soft white bread crumbs

. . . .

½ cup salad oil

The Night Before
Preparation and Cooking Time: 30 min.

Sauté scallions in butter until they turn soft. Add shellfish, sauté gently for 2 min. Add sherry, simmer for 1 min. longer.

Turn heat up and boil until most of liquid evaporates. Remove from heat, add oregano, and set aside. Lightly beat egg yolk and cream together in a large bowl. Set aside.

In a saucepan, melt butter, add flour, cook and stir for 1 min. Slowly add hot milk, beating with a wire whisk as you add it. Cook over high heat for 1 min. Add Swiss cheese and pepper and remove from heat. Add this sauce to the bowl of egg yolk and cream by beating in a little at a time with a wire whisk.

Return to saucepan and cook for a minute or two. Remove from heat and add shellfish. Place a piece of waxed paper on a large plate. Drop large spoonfuls of fish mixture onto waxed paper, forming round or oval patties about 1 inch thick. Cover with second piece of waxed paper. Put in freezer section of refrigerator for an hour or two; the patties should get firm enough to handle. Spread flour and bread crumbs out on two large plates for later use.

When patties are firm, remove from refrigerator. Beat eggs and oil together. Coat each piece with flour, then with egg, then with bread crumbs. Then go back again, this time rolling each piece in egg and bread crumbs only. Cover, refrigerate.

Before Serving

Preparation Time: 1 min.   Cooking Time: 10 to 15 min.

Heat oil in large skillet (375° for an electric skillet). Fry patties until browned on both sides. Drain on paper towels and serve.   Serves 4

Salmon Vinaigrette

This salmon is served cold. We like to serve it accompanied by parsley mayonnaise (page 89).

1 lb. salmon steak, cut at least ¾ inch thick	⅛ teaspoon pepper
	1 bay leaf
1 medium onion, quartered	2 cups vinegar
¼ teaspoon salt	4 cups water
¼ teaspoon sugar	

The Night Before

Preparation Time: 5 min.   Cooking Time: 50 min.

Put all ingredients except the salmon steak into a pot and and cook over a high flame for 25 min. Heat the oven to 325°. Pour some of the liquid into the bottom of a roasting pan or a casserole which is large enough for the salmon steaks to be placed flat in it. Lay the salmon steaks gently in the liquid and pour the rest of liquid around the pieces of fish. Bake, uncovered, for 25 min. Remove from oven, cool, cover and refrigerate the dish.

44

Before Serving

Preparation Time: 1 min.

Carefully remove the salmon steaks from the liquid, using a spatula.   *Serves 4*

Baked Salmon Casserole

1 can (1 lb.) salmon
3 slices white bread
½ medium onion, sliced
2 eggs
2 tablespoons butter
¼ cup celery leaves

3 sprigs parsley
½ teaspoon salt
¼ teaspoon dry mustard
⅛ teaspoon Tabasco
¾ cup milk

The Night Before

Preparation Time: 15 min.

(Our calculated preparation time is based on the use of an electric blender. If you do not have one, the preparation time will be 25 to 30 min.)

If using a blender, tear each slice of white bread into 6 or 7 pieces and place one slice at a time into the blender. Blend for 3 or 4 seconds and pour crumbs into a large mixing bowl before blending the next slice. If you have no blender, tear or cut the bread into the smallest pieces you can manage.

Place all the remaining ingredients in the blender and blend on high speed for about ½ min. Pour blended mixture over bread crumbs and mix well. Cover and refrigerate. If you have no blender, beat the eggs and chop the celery leaves, parsley, and onion very fine before adding to the bread crumbs. Then add milk, salmon, melted butter, and seasonings and mix well.

Before Serving

Preparation Time: 2 min.   *Cooking Time:* 50 min.

Heat oven to 375°. Butter the inside of a 1-quart casserole and pour salmon mixture into it. Bake, uncovered, for 50 min.

(Parsley mayonnaise—page 89—goes well with this. Or, if you prefer a hot sauce, heat 1 can cream of celery or cream of mushroom soup with ¼ cup milk just before serving.)

Serves 4

Filet of Sole in Parsley Sauce

¼ lb. (1 stick) butter	3 tablespoons chopped scallions
2 tablespoons lemon juice	1 teaspoon salt
3 tablespoons chopped parsley	⅛ teaspoon thyme

• • • • • • • • • • • • •

2 lbs. filet of sole

The Night Before

Preparation Time: 15 min.

Cream the butter in a small, heavy saucepan. Blend in lemon juice, parsley, scallions, salt, and thyme. Cover saucepan with a tight-fitting cover or with foil and refrigerate.

Before Serving

Preparation Time: 5 min.   *Cooking Time:* 20 min.

Heat oven to 350°. While oven is heating, heat the sauce slowly on top of the stove. Pour half the heated sauce into an oven-to-table serving dish. Place the filets of sole in the dish and pour the remaining sauce over them. Bake for approximately 20 min. (Baking time will depend on the thickness of the filets. Test for doneness by flaking the fish with a fork; it is done when it flakes easily.)

Serves 4

Filet of Sole in Sherry and Cream Sauce

2 lbs. sole or flounder filets
2 scallions, chopped
2 tablespoons butter
¾ cup dry sherry (or other dry white wine, if you prefer)
¾ cup cold water
2 egg yolks
Scant ¾ cup heavy cream

3 tablespoons butter
¼ cup flour
¾ cup milk
¼ teaspoon salt
¼ teaspoon lemon juice
3 tablespoons grated Swiss cheese
Extra butter (for dotting)

The Night Before

Preparation and Cooking Time: 35 min.

Preheat oven to 350°. Butter a baking dish that can be used on top of the stove, in the oven, under the broiler, and for serving. Spread half the scallions on bottom of dish. Fold each filet in half and place filets, side by side, over scallions. Spread rest of scallions on top of filets. Dot with 2 tablespoons butter. Mix sherry and water together and pour over fish. Cook over medium heat on top of stove until liquid simmers—takes about 5 min. Remove from heat.

Place a piece of waxed paper directly on top of fish. Bake in 350° oven for 10 min. While the fish is baking, start preparing the sauce.

Beat egg yolks and ½ cup cream together in a large bowl until they are well blended. Set aside. Melt 3 tablespoons butter in a saucepan, add flour, and cook over low heat, stirring constantly, until mixture thickens and bubbles. Remove from heat.

Remove fish from oven and pour off liquid, reserving 1 cup. Add reserved liquid to butter-flour mixture. Stir vigorously, then stir in milk. Return to heat, bring to boil, and boil for 1 min., stirring all the while. Remove from heat. Add this sauce, a tablespoonful at a time, to the bowl containing the egg yolks and cream. Beat in each spoonful thoroughly (a wire whisk is helpful here) before adding the next—this will give you the smooth consistency that could not be achieved otherwise. Return the sauce to the pan and, stirring constantly, bring to boil over fairly high heat, then continue to boil for 1 min. Stir in remaining ¼ cup cream to thin sauce. Add salt and lemon juice, taste, and correct seasoning if necessary.

Pour sauce over fish. Top with grated Swiss cheese and dot with butter. Cover and refrigerate.

Before Serving

Preparation Time: 2 min.   *Cooking Time:* 12 to 14 min.

Preheat broiler. Place uncovered dish on top of stove and cook over medium heat until sauce begins to bubble. Then put under broiler, 4 inches from heat, until top of sauce browns.   *Serves 4*

Pat's Fish Stew

This dish involves quite a lot of chopping but if you do it at the times indicated in the recipe, the total preparation time is not too horrendous. And the result is, to put it mildly, glamorous.

½ cup salad oil
1 cup flour
2 medium onions, chopped
3 stalks celery, chopped
1 small green pepper, chopped
1 clove garlic, chopped
1 small can tomato paste
1 teaspoon Worcestershire sauce

1 can (10 oz.) tomatoes
4 cups hot water
1½ cups parsley, chopped
3 scallions, including green tops, chopped
¼ lb. (1 stick) butter or margarine
4 thin slices of lemon

. . . .

1½ lbs. red snapper or pompano, boned

1½ teaspoons salt
1¼ cups Burgundy

48

The Night Before

Preparation Time: 35 min.   Cooking Time: 15 min.
                                          (in addition to preparation time)

Chop the onions, green pepper, celery, and garlic. Heat the salad oil in a very large (6 quart) casserole over a low flame. Add the flour gradually, stirring, until the mixture is thick, smooth, and a very light brown. Add onions, celery, garlic, and green pepper. Mix well. Add tomato paste, Worcestershire sauce, and tomatoes and cook for 5 min. Gradually add hot water, stirring after each addition. When all water has been added, simmer for 10 min. Meanwhile, chop the scallions and parsley.

After the mixture has simmered for 10 min., add the scallions, parsley, lemon, and butter. Stir and let simmer for 15 min. Cool and refrigerate.

Before Serving

Preparation Time: 3 min.   Cooking Time: 35 min.

Reheat the sauce for 5 min. Meanwhile, cut the fish into pieces about 3 inches square. Add the fish and salt to the sauce and stir gently. Cook for 10 min.; then add the wine and let the stew simmer for 20 min. more. Remove the lemon slices before serving. (Rice goes well with this and may be prepared while the stew is simmering.)   *Serves 6*

Souperb: A Main-Dish Fish Chowder

This New England style chowder combines two virtues not often found in one dish—it is exquisitely flavored, yet hearty enough to satisfy even the most ravenous appetites. A meal planned around this soup should contain little else—a fruit salad, some crusty French bread, and a very light, cold dessert nicely complement the chowder, making a more than ample meal.

5 or 6 oz. piece salt pork, cut into chunks	3 tablespoons butter
2 cups water	3 tablespoons flour
2 onions, coarsely chopped	2 cups milk
3 large potatoes, diced	Black pepper

. . . .

1 lb. frozen cod filets (other fish, fresh or frozen, may be used successfully)
Additional milk, if necessary

The Night Before
Preparation Time: 15 min.   *Cooking Time:* 40 min.

Place the chunks of salt pork into a heavy, 4-quart pot and cook over medium high heat for 15 min. to render part of the fat. Meanwhile, chop the onions, dice the potatoes into rather large chunks, and prepare this white sauce, which will be used later to thicken the chowder: melt the butter in a saucepan, stir in flour and cook until smooth; add milk, cooking and stirring until mixture thickens. Remove from heat and reserve.

Add the 2 cups water to the salt pork and melted fat. Bring to a fast boil, then simmer for 5 min. Add onions, cover, and simmer for 10 min. Add potatoes, cover, and simmer for 10 min. more. Stir white sauce into the soup and cook together for a minute or two. Season to taste with black pepper. Cover and refrigerate.

Before Serving
Preparation Time: 1 min.   *Cooking Time:* 15 to 20 min.

Place frozen fish filets on top of chowder, cover, and simmer for 15 to 20 minutes. The cooking time here depends on the type and thickness of the fish used, and on whether it is fresh or frozen. (The fish is done if it flakes easily when tested with a fork.) If the chowder seems a bit too thick for your taste, thin it with milk.   *Serves 4*

See also: Spaghetti with Oyster Sauce (page 67).

50

□ FOWL □

Many of these recipes call for a 3 to 3½ lb. chicken. Since you will be using fairly short cooking times, it is important not to buy an emaciated stewing hen. Your safest bet is what is known as a broiler-fryer—a somewhat misleading name, since this type of young chicken takes well to many kinds of cooking other than broiling or frying.

Chinese Fried Chicken

3½ lb. frying chicken, cut in parts	2 tablespoons molasses
½ cup honey	½ cup soy sauce
¼ cup vinegar	2 cups water

. . . .

¾ cup sifted flour	2 cups salad oil
1 tablespoon salt	

The Night Before
Preparation Time: 10 min.   *Cooking Time:* 50 min.

Place chicken and 2 cups water in a pot. Cover, bring to a boil, then reduce heat, and simmer for 45 min. Drain the chicken, rinse it in cold water, and dry with paper towels.

Make a marinade of the honey, vinegar, molasses, and soy sauce. Brush the chicken with the marinade and place the chicken in a large bowl, pouring the remaining marinade over it. Refrigerate. Turn the pieces over in the marinade once the next morning.

Before Serving
Preparation and Cooking Time: 10 min.

If you're using an electric skillet, heat it to 375°; then add the oil and allow it to heat to the same temperature. If you're still cooking without an electric skillet (and we don't quite understand why you should be at this point), heat the oil in a heavy skillet or deep fat fryer to 375°.

While the oil is heating, put the flour and salt in a paper bag; add the chicken pieces, a few at a time, and shake the bag vigorously to coat the chicken with the flour. Fry the chicken until golden brown. This will take only 2 to 3 min. Drain on paper towels. *Serves 4*

Chicken and Rice Elayne

This dish is susceptible to variation. If you're pressed for time, you can use canned chicken and chicken broth. If you want to make it in tremendous quantities (and it's an ideal buffet dish for a crowd) and economy is important, leave out the chicken altogether and double the frankfurters.

FOR PREPARING THE CHICKEN

1 3-lb. chicken, cut in parts	1 onion, quartered
1 tablespoon salt	3 sprigs parsley
¼ teaspoon pepper	4 cups water
1 stalk of celery, with leaves	

FOR THE CASSEROLE

½ cup raw rice	1 green pepper, diced
1 tablespoon butter	1 can (3 oz.) chopped mush-
1 clove garlic, crushed	rooms
1 medium onion, chopped	4 frankfurters, cut in chunks
1 can (1 lb.) tomatoes	1 teaspoon salt
1½ cups canned spaghetti sauce	¾ teaspoon oregano

The Night Before

Preparation Time: 25 to 30 min.   *Cooking Time:* 1¼ hrs.
(exclusive of preparation time)

Cook the chicken in 4 cups water with the salt, pepper, celery, quartered onion, and parsley for about 1 hr. Remove from pot and cut chicken in bite-size pieces. Reserve 1 cup of the broth.

Brown the rice in the butter until golden, stirring constantly. Add the cup of chicken broth, stir, and then add all other ingredients. Simmer for 15 min. over a low flame and turn into an ungreased casserole. Let cool and refrigerate overnight.

Before Serving

Preparation Time: 1 min.   *Cooking Time:* 1 hr.

Heat oven to 350°. Bake casserole, uncovered, for 1 hr.

Serves 6

Chicken Breasts Crème Rouge

4 chicken breasts
1 large onion, coarsely chopped
¾ cup chicken broth (or 1 chicken bouillon cube dissolved in ¾ cup boiling water)

3 tablespoons olive oil
1 clove garlic, minced
1 green pepper, diced
1 teaspoon salt
2 tablespoons paprika
1 cup canned tomatoes, **drained**

. . . .

4 tablespoons flour
4 tablespoons light cream

½ cup sour cream

The Night Before

Preparation Time: 15 min.   *Cooking Time:* 30 to 40 min.

In a large, heavy skillet or Dutch oven, sauté the chopped onion in the olive oil until golden—4 or 5 min. over a moderately low flame. Meanwhile, mix together the broth, garlic, green pepper, salt, paprika, and tomatoes. Add these to the onions, cover the skillet, and cook gently for 10 min. Add the chicken breasts, cover, and simmer for 30 to 40 min., or until tender. Remove chicken and let cool before covering

53

and refrigerating. Measure off 1½ cups of the sauce left in the pan, let cool, and refrigerate separately.

Before Serving

Preparation Time: 6 min.   *Cooking Time:* 15 min.
(of which the last 5 min. are in-kitchen time)

Place chicken and sauce in skillet, or, ideally, in a stove-to-table type pot, and heat through. This should take about 10 min. Remove the chicken breasts. Mix the flour and cream together to make a smooth paste, add it to the sauce in the pan, and stir over medium heat until sauce is thickened and smooth. Lower flame, add sour cream, and cook just until heated through. Return chicken to the sauce (or pour sauce over chicken in serving dish) and serve.   *Serves 4*

Spanish Chicken

1 chicken (3½ lbs.) cut in serv-
    ing pieces
¼ cup olive oil
1 cup uncooked rice
1 medium onion, chopped
1 small green pepper, chopped

2 cloves garlic, chopped
3 tomatoes, cut in quarters
1 can (8½ oz.) green peas
1 tablespoon salt
1½ cups water

The Night Before

Preparation Time: 35 min.   *Cooking Time:* 30 min.

Heat oil in a heavy skillet (350° for an electric skillet) or a heavy pot. Sauté chicken until lightly browned. Remove chicken to a platter. Sauté the rice in the same skillet or pot, stirring constantly, until rice is golden. Add the onion, garlic, and green pepper and cook, stirring frequently, for 5 min. Remove from heat and stir in the tomatoes, salt, and green peas. Place this mixture and the chicken in a casserole and pour the water over the top. It is important to be sure that the rice is covered by the water or is under the tomatoes so that it has sufficient liquid to ensure adequate cooking.

Place the casserole, covered, in a 400° oven. Bake for ½ hr. Cool and refrigerate.

Before Serving

Preparation Time: 1 min.   *Cooking Time:* 40 min.

Heat oven to 400°. Check casserole to be sure rice is still in liquid and not on top of the chicken. Add a little water if necessary. Bake, uncovered, for 40 min.   *Serves 4 to 5*

Chicken Cacciatore

1 chicken (3 to 3½ lbs.), cut in   2 cloves garlic, minced
   serving pieces   2 teaspoons salt
⅓ cup salad oil   ¼ teaspoon pepper
2 medium onions, sliced   1 teaspoon celery seed
1 can (1 lb.) Italian tomatoes   1 teaspoon oregano
1 can (8 oz.) tomato sauce

The Night Before

Preparation Time: 30 min.   *Cooking Time:* 1¼ hrs.
                                             (including preparation time)

Brown the chicken in hot salad oil. While it is browning, slice the onions and mince the garlic. As the chicken browns, remove it from the skillet and place in a large saucepan or a top-of-the-stove casserole. Place the onions in the oil and cook until golden. Remove the onions with a slotted spoon and add them to the chicken. Drain the fat from the skillet. (If reserving fat for use in another dish makes you feel thrifty and virtuous, save it; if, however, discarding cooking fat makes you feel *slender* and virtuous, go right ahead.) Use the same skillet for mixing all the remaining ingredients. Pour the sauce over the chicken. Cover the saucepan or casserole and cook over a low flame for 15 min. Then uncover the pan and cook for another half hour, turning the chicken pieces over occasionally. Cool slightly and refrigerate, covered.

Before Serving

Preparation Time: 2 min.   Cooking Time: 20 min.

Skim off any fat that has risen to the top of the sauce. Cook, uncovered, over a low flame for 20 min., turning chicken pieces once or twice.

Serves 4

Chicken and Wild Rice Casserole

No dish using cream, mushrooms, and wild rice could by any stretch of the imagination be called an economy dish. If, however, you feel the need to rationalize this one, it does have its economical aspects. For one thing, it needs no accompaniment other than salad, rolls, and a light dessert, so that the total cost of a company dinner that will make your reputation as a cook is not too high. In addition, you will end up with a pot of chicken soup which can form the core of an inexpensive meal for later in the week. Chicken Egg Drop Soup or is Chicken Soup with Matzo Balls (pages 124–125) are two good ways of using your leftover soup.

If you need any further rationalization, we point out that this is the recipe we have wearily typed over and over again for guests who wanted it and, on one occasion, dictated the whole thing over the phone to a harried mother who decided it was just the thing she wanted to make in large quantities for her daughter's engagement party.

FOR PREPARING THE CHICKEN

1 chicken, about 4 lbs., cut in parts
1 large onion, quartered

1 carrot, peeled
1 stalk celery
3 tablespoons salt

56

FOR THE CASSEROLE

1 cup raw wild rice
¼ lb. butter
¼ cup flour
1 can (6 oz.) sliced mushrooms
1½ cups light cream

1 small can pimento
½ cup chopped onion
2 tablespoons chopped parsley
2 teaspoons salt

. . . .

¼ cup slivered, blanched almonds

The Night Before

Preparation Time: 25 min.   *Cooking Time:* 1¼ hrs.

Place chicken in a large pot, generously covering it with water. Add the quartered onion, carrot, celery, and the 3 tablespoons salt. Cook for 1 hr. While the chicken is cooking, cook the wild rice according to package directions. You can also chop the onion and pimento and drain the mushrooms, reserving the liquid.

When the chicken is done, remove it from the pot, reserving the broth. Let it cool slightly and remove the meat from the bones, cutting it in ½-inch pieces. Cook the onion in the butter until tender but not brown. Remove from stove; stir in flour. Add enough chicken broth to the mushroom liquid to make 1½ cups. Add this liquid gradually to the flour-butter-onion mixture while heating over a medium flame. Add the cream and cook, stirring, until thick. Remove from flame and add rice, chicken, parsley, pimento, mushrooms, and salt. Turn into casserole and store in refrigerator.

Before Serving

Preparation Time: 2 min.   *Cooking Time:* 30 min.

Heat oven to 350°. Remove casserole from refrigerator, stir contents with a spoon, and sprinkle almonds on top. Place in oven, uncovered, for 30 min.   *Serves 6*

Lickin' Chicken

4 boned chicken breasts
½ cup olive oil
½ cup Worcestershire sauce
¼ teaspoon curry powder

⅛ teaspoon thyme
⅛ teaspoon tarragon
¼ teaspoon salt

The Night Before
Preparation Time: 5 min.

Combine olive oil, Worcestershire, and seasonings. Place chicken breasts in baking dish, turn to coat well, cover, and refrigerate. Turn chicken in marinade once before going to bed, and once again in the morning.

Before Serving
Preparation Time: 4 to 5 min.   *Cooking Time:* 1 hr., 5 min.

Preheat oven to 350°. Place covered baking dish in oven. Bake for 1 hr., basting with marinade once or twice. Remove from oven, run under broiler for 2 min. on each side, and serve.   *Serves 4*

Duck with Apricots

5 lb. duck, cut in parts
1½ teaspoons salt
¼ teaspoon pepper

3 cloves garlic
8 oz. canned apricot juice
¾ cup dried apricots

The Night Before
Preparation Time: 10 min.   *Cooking Time:* 1 hr.

Heat oven to 325°. Sprinkle duck with salt and pepper and place, skin side up, on a rack in a baking pan. Bake 1 hr.

While duck is baking, boil the apricots for 15 to 20 min. and discard water. Mash garlic and mix garlic, apricot juice, and apricots together.

When duck has baked for 1 hr., drain off all fat. Remove

the rack and put duck in bottom of pan, pouring the apricot
mixture over it. Cover and refrigerate.

Before Serving

Preparation Time: 1 min.   *Cooking Time:* 35 min.

Heat oven to 325°, and bake, uncovered, for 35 min. *Serves 6*

□   □

Tongue with Piquant Sauce

1 smoked beef tongue (3 lbs.)	⅓ cup brown sugar
1 onion, quartered	¼ cup wine vinegar
¼ cup gingersnap crumbs	1 cup beef bouillon
⅓ cup white raisins	

The Night Before

Preparation Time: 12 min.   *Cooking Time:* 3 hrs.
(if your beef tongue weighs either less or more than 3 lbs., allow 1 hr. per lb. for cooking time)

Place tongue in a large kettle and cover with water. Add the quartered onion and bring the water to a boil. Simmer until done—1 hr. per pound of tongue.

Prepare the sauce by reducing gingersnap crackers to crumbs in the blender or crushing the crackers with a rolling pin; then place the crumbs in a saucepan with the raisins, sugar, vinegar, and bouillon. Stir and let simmer for 10 min. Cool and refrigerate, covered.

When tongue is done, remove it from the pot and let it cool. The skin can then be removed easily by cutting through the underside and peeling the skin off. Remove any small bones from the back and any excess fat. Wrap in waxed paper or foil and refrigerate.

Before Serving

Preparation Time: 4 min.   *Cooking Time:* 5 to 6 min.

Reheat sauce. Meanwhile, slice tongue into quarter inch slices. Serve the tongue slices cold and pass the hot sauce to be spooned over it.

Serves 8 (If you're serving fewer people, you will have enough tongue left over for luncheon sandwiches.)

Monday's Oxtail Ragout

This is called "Monday's" Ragout because, while the time needed in preparation is not great, the combination of the marinating time and the cooking time is too much for a single evening unless you start earlier than is probably convenient. If you plan this for Monday's dinner, however, the time problem disappears. The meat can be marinated Sunday afternoon when you finish the lunch dishes or while you're putting the final touches on your Sunday evening meal. The cooking can then be left for after dinner.

3 oxtails, cut in 2-inch pieces	¼ cup flour
2 cups Burgundy	1 teaspoon paprika
2 large onions, chopped	1 clove garlic, minced
1 carrot, chopped	1½ cups tomato purée
10 whole peppercorns	6 carrots
4 teaspoons salt	3 cups water
3 tablespoons salad oil	

The Day Before

Preparation Time: 35 min.   *Cookin ; Time:* 2 hrs.

Place the oxtails in a deep bowl and cover with a marinade made of the chopped onions, chopped carrot, peppercorns, 1 teaspoon salt, and the Burgundy. Cover and refrigerate for 3 to 5 hrs., turning every once in a while.

Pare the 6 carrots and cut them diagonally. Wrap in waxed paper or a plastic bag and refrigerate.

When the oxtails have been marinated for the convenient length of time, remove them from the marinade and dry them on a triple thickness of paper towel. Heat the salad oil in a Dutch oven and brown the oxtails well on all sides. Stir in the flour, then add the marinade, the remaining 3 teaspoons salt, paprika, garlic, tomato purée, and the water. Stir and cover. Simmer for 2 hrs. Cool slightly and refrigerate.

61

Preparation Time: 2 min.   *Cooking Time:* 1 hr.

Remove the fat from the surface of the ragout. Pour the carrots into the ragout. Stir, cover, and simmer for 1 hr.

(This goes well with either noodles or mashed potatoes. If your family, like ours, likes to pour the extra ragout gravy over their noodles or potatoes, don't add any butter when you cook them.)   *Serves 4*

Calf's Liver Dijon

In anticipation of your skepticism when you read this recipe, we'll assure you that neither we nor the typesetter has gone berserk. Admittedly, the combination of ingredients is unusual, if not downright unlikely—mustard *and* garlic *and* onions *and* parsley? On liver? Believe it or not, the final result is not only delicious but also subtle. Be brave. Try it.

1½ to 2 lbs. calf's liver, thickly sliced (about ⅜ to ½ inch)
½ cup flour
1 tablespoon salad oil
3 tablespoons butter
¼ cup Dijon mustard (a prepared French mustard)

3 tablespoons parsley, finely minced
1 scallion, finely minced
1 small clove garlic, crushed
8 to 12 slices very fresh white bread, trimmed of crusts and crumbed in blender

· · · · · ·   · · · · · · ·

5 tablespoons butter ⎤
2 tablespoons salad oil ⎦   skillet method
    or
7 tablespoons melted butter   broiler method

The Night Before
Preparation and Cooking Time: 17 min.

Mix flour, salt, and pepper and spread out on paper towel or flat dish. Heat butter and oil in large skillet over high heat. Coat liver with flour. Sauté briefly until lightly browned—

about 1 to 1½ min. on each side. Remove liver from skillet and set aside.

Mix mustard, parsley, scallion, and garlic together; blend well. Little by little, add the fat remaining in the skillet to this mixture—beat in ½ teaspoon fat at a time. This mixture shouldn't get watery—it must remain thick enough to spread over the liver; if using all the fat would make it too thin, stop adding fat.

Prepare bread crumbs by trimming crusts from 8 to 12 slices (depends on thickness) of *very* fresh, soft, white bread. Crumb the bread in the electric blender (one slice at a time). You should have 3 or 3½ cups bread crumbs. Spread bread crumbs out on a flat surface.

Spread mustard mixture over liver slices, then dip in bread crumbs, coating well. If necessary, press crumbs down lightly with your fingers or with a small spatula. Place liver on a plate with waxed paper in between layers of liver slices. Cover plate with waxed paper or foil.

Before Serving
Preparation Time: 4 min.   *Cooking Time:* 5 to 8 min.

Skillet Method: Melt butter and oil in skillet until fairly hot. Sauté liver slices until covering is nicely browned on each side.

Broiler Method: Preheat broiler. Melt butter in small saucepan. Broil for 2 to 3 min. on each side, pouring half the butter over each side before broiling.   *Serves 4*

Baked Bean Casserole

2 cans (1 lb. each) baked beans
½ cup ketchup
¼ cup molasses
¼ cup brown sugar
¼ cup minced onion

¼ cup green pepper, finely chopped
¾ lb. sliced Canadian bacon (or 5 frankfurters, sliced)
1 orange, sliced

63

The Night Before

Preparation Time: 8 min.

Place the beans in a shallow casserole. Add all other ingredients except the meat and the orange. Mix well. Lay the Canadian bacon around the edges, overlapping the slices. If you are using frankfurters instead, place the slices in rows around the edges. Place the orange slices in an overlapping row down the center of the casserole. Cover tightly with aluminum foil and refrigerate.

Before Serving

Preparation Time: 1 min.   *Cooking Time:* 35 min.

Heat oven to 375°. Bake the casserole, uncovered, for 35 min.   *Serves 5*

Double Duty Recipe: Sweet and Sour Cabbage Soup—Unstuffed Stuffed Cabbage

Stuffed cabbage seemed a "natural" for this book, because it's one of those dishes that demands night-before cooking for the sake of flavor. We had two problems, though: (1) We'd seen people devote a whole evening to preparing it, and since we were not about to spend, or suggest that *you* spend, 4 or 5 hours on one meal, we had to find a simpler way. Shirley Greenwald solved that one for us with her clever notion of leaving the cabbage *un*stuffed—everything is there, the cabbage and the meat are simmered in the sweet and sour sauce, there's no difference in taste, and the whole thing takes 10 minutes to prepare. (2) We needed a good recipe for sweet and sour sauce—the kind Mother used to make. Being the resourceful souls that we are, we took the problem to Dorothy

Freeman, who happens to be Mother to half of us, and she gave us her marvelous recipe for sweet and sour cabbage soup.

As given, the recipe is for unstuffed stuffed cabbage. If you wish to prepare cabbage soup instead, omit the starred ingredients and decrease the tomato sauce to ¾ cup.

2 lb. head green cabbage	½ cup vinegar
*1 lb. chopped chuck	¾ cup light brown sugar
*1 egg	2 tablespoons lemon juice
*¼ lb. raw rice	1½ cups water
*¼ teaspoon salt	1 apple, cored, pared, and cut
1 can (1 lb.) stewed tomatoes	into chunks
1 cup tomato sauce (see note above)	1 small package (1½ oz.) seedless raisins

The Night Before

Preparation Time: 7 to 10 min.   *Cooking Time:* 2½ hrs.

Cut head of cabbage into quarters, then cut quarters into chunks, shreds, strips, or whatever. Place cabbage into a 6-quart pot. Then add tomatoes, tomato sauce, vinegar, brown sugar, lemon juice, water and apple. If you're making soup, your preparations are over now. Just cover the pot and simmer for 2½ hrs., adding the raisins 45 min. before it's done. If you're cooking this as a main dish, cover and cook over medium-high heat while you prepare the meat mixture. (This will give the cabbage a chance to get slightly soft, so that you can push it down and make room for the meat to float on top of the sauce.)

Mix chopped chuck with egg, raw rice, and salt. Form into meatballs; put meatballs on top of sauce. Cover pot, lower heat, and simmer very gently for 2½ hrs., stirring occasionally. About 45 min. before the end of the cooking time, add raisins.

Before Serving

Preparation Time: ½ min.   *Cooking Time:* 15 to 20 min.

Place covered pot on top of stove and cook over low heat for 15 or 20 min.

If made with meat, this is excellent to serve over rice.

Serves 4

Danny's Spaghetti Sauce

This is known as "Danny's Sauce" despite the fact that it was a staple of the newlywed Zavins' Friday night open house years before young Danny was born. It acquired its name this way: one night everyone, including the puzzled cook, agreed that the spaghetti sauce was bland and not as good as usual. Investigation proved that Danny had, for many months, habitually tasted and added seasoning to the sauce every time he passed the kitchen while the sauce was cooking. (This also explained why the same recipe seemed to produce considerably *less* sauce than we had been accustomed to having.) On this particular occasion, the sauce had been cooked after our man-for-all-seasonings had gone to bed. At any rate, we like Danny's additions. You can adjust the seasoning according to your taste or that of your own tasters.

1 lb. chopped chuck	1 can tomato paste
1 medium onion, chopped	2 teaspoons oregano
1 clove garlic, chopped	1 teaspoon sugar
1 tablespoon olive oil	½ teaspoon garlic salt
1 can (1 lb.) Italian plum to- matoes	1 to 2 teaspoons salt
	Dash pepper

. . . .

1 package (1 lb.) spaghetti

The Night Before

Preparation Time: 7 min.   *Cooking Time:* 30 min.

Chop onion and garlic and cook slowly in oil until yellow but not crisp. Add beef and cook, stirring, until browned. Add tomatoes, tomato paste, and seasonings. Cook, uncovered, over low flame for 20 min., stirring once or twice.

Before Serving

Preparation Time: 5 min.   *Cooking Time:* 15 min.

Cook spaghetti according to package directions. Skim fat from sauce and heat slowly for 15 min., stirring occasionally.

Serves 5

Spaghetti with Oyster Sauce

¼ cup salad oil	3 stalks celery, chopped
¼ cup flour	1 green pepper, chopped
1 large onion, chopped	2 cloves garlic, chopped
1 can (1 lb.) tomato sauce	1½ cups hot water

. . . .

1 lb. frozen, canned, or fresh, shucked oysters	½ teaspoon salt
	1 lb. spaghetti

The Night Before

Preparation Time: 15 min.   *Cooking Time:* 2 hrs.

Chop the onion, celery, green pepper, and garlic before you begin cooking.

Heat the salad oil in a fairly large saucepan. Add flour gradually, stirring constantly. Add the onion, tomato sauce, green pepper, celery, and garlic. Mix well. Add the 1½ cups hot water gradually, stirring after each addition. Simmer for 2 hrs. This is a fairly thick sauce and is best cooked over an asbestos mat or other flame shield. You can, if you like, start the cooking in the top part of your double boiler and put it over hot water in the bottom part for the 2-hour simmering period. If you do cook it directly over the flame, keep the flame very low and stir frequently to avoid scorching.

When the sauce has simmered for 2 hrs., cool it slightly, cover, and refrigerate in the pan in which it was cooked.

Before Serving

Preparation Time: 5 min.   *Cooking Time:* 30 min.

Cook spaghetti according to package directions. While water for spaghetti is boiling, heat sauce over very low flame for 10 min. Add drained oysters and salt and continue simmering for 20 min.

Place drained spaghetti in a large serving bowl. Pour oyster sauce over the spaghetti and mix well.   *Serves 5 to 6*

Mrs. Albini's Baked Lasagna

Every time our friends, Emilia and Thayer Taylor, have a baby, Emilia's mother, Marion Albini, comes down from Gloversville for a couple of weeks to help out. At some time before she goes home she cooks what she deprecatingly calls "just an old-fashioned Italian dinner" for a few of the Taylors' lucky friends. As a result, these may be the only babies in the world whose birth announcements make the recipients lick their chops in happy anticipation.

Neither of us can duplicate the total effect of Marion's sumptuous dinner. We have, however, had wonderful luck both with this lasagna and with the roasted peppers (see page 91 for the recipe).

THE SAUCE

¾ lb. pork or beef, cut in large chunks
½ lb. Italian sweet sausage
1 tablespoon shortening
1 small onion, chopped

1 clove garlic, chopped
1 tablespoon basil
1 teaspoon oregano
2 cans tomato paste
2 cups water

THE LASAGNA

½ lb. lasagna noodles
1 lb. ricotta or cottage cheese

1 lb. mozzarella cheese, sliced
¼ lb. grated Parmesan cheese

The Night Before

Preparation Time: 30 min.   *Cooking Time:* 2 hrs., 45 min.

Melt shortening in large heavy pot. Add meat and sausage and cook slowly until well browned. Add onion and garlic and cook until golden. Add basil, oregano, and 2 cups water, or more if 2 cups won't quite cover the meat. Allow to come to a boil and then add tomato paste and stir. Lower flame, cover, and simmer for 2½ hrs. Stir occasionally and add water if needed.

During the last 15 min. in which the sauce cooks, prepare the lasagna according to package directions. Heat oven to 350°.

When the sauce is done, remove the meat from the sauce and place meat in top of a double boiler; cover and refrigerate.

In a deep rectangular baking pan or casserole, place a few spoonfuls of sauce. Over this, place one layer of lasagna. Cover with dabs of ricotta, slices of mozzarella, Parmesan cheese, and one quarter of the sauce. Start again with a layer of lasagna, adding the other ingredients in the same order. Make 3 or 4 layers of this. The last layer should consist only of lasagna, Parmesan cheese, and sauce. Bake, uncovered, for 15 min. Remove from oven, let stand for 15 min., cover and refrigerate.

Before Serving

Preparation Time: 2 min.   *Cooking Time:* 20 min.

Heat the lasagna casserole at 350° for 15 to 20 min. Let it stand 5 to 10 min. before cutting and serving. While the lasagna is baking, heat the meat in the top of the double boiler. Serve it separately. (Someone to whom we once gave this recipe made a mistake and put the meat in the lasagna casserole along with the sauce. It came out fine.)   *Serves 6*

Second-Best Lasagna

We freely admit that this is not as good as Mrs. Albini's lasagna, but it *is* good and can be prepared in less time. We use Mrs. Albini's recipe when we have a long evening for cooking and this one when time is short.

1 lb. chopped chuck	½ lb. sliced mozzarella cheese
1 can (1 lb.) Italian tomatoes	½ lb. ricotta or cottage cheese
1 can (8 oz.) tomato sauce	Enough lasagna noodles to
2 crushed cloves of garlic	make 3 layers in your pan
2 teaspoons salt	(usually a little over ½ lb.)
½ teaspoon pepper	

. . . .

½ cup grated Parmesan cheese

The Night Before

Preparation Time: 18 min.   *Cooking Time:* 45 min.

Put chopped chuck and salt in a saucepan and brown thoroughly, stirring. Add the garlic and pepper and simmer slowly for 10 min. Add tomatoes and tomato sauce, mix, cover, and simmer for 30 min.

While the sauce is cooking, cook the lasagna according to the directions on the box. Drain, rinse with cold water, and drain again.

When sauce is finished, pour one quarter of it over the bottom of a baking dish (12"x8"x2" is a good size). Arrange a layer of lasagna over the sauce. Top with a layer of mozzarella pieces alternated with spoonfuls of ricotta. Top with a third of the remaining sauce. Repeat the layers, ending with a layer of meat sauce. Cover and refrigerate.

Before Serving

Preparation Time: 2 min.   *Cooking Time:* 30 min.

Heat oven to 350°. Sprinkle Parmesan cheese over top of lasagna and bake, uncovered, for 30 min. Let the casserole stand for at least 5 min. after you have taken it out of the oven before you cut it.

Note: This dish takes well to freezing. If, however, you are taking it from freezer to oven without thawing, increase the cooking time to 40 min.)   *Serves 6*

Cannelloni with Cheese Sauce

1¾ cups diced cooked chicken
1 lb. lasagna noodles
2 tablespoons butter
2 tablespoons olive oil
1 clove garlic, minced
½ small onion, finely chopped

1 egg
2 tablespoons heavy cream or evaporated milk
¼ teaspoon thyme
½ teaspoon salt

THE CHEESE SAUCE

3 tablespoons butter
3 tablespoons flour
1½ cups chicken broth
¾ cup heavy cream or evaporated milk

Salt and pepper to taste
1 cup grated Parmesan cheese

The Night Before
Preparation and Cooking Time: 25 min.

Cook lasagna in 6 quarts of boiling water for 5 to 7 min. Drain, wipe noodles with a dry cloth, and lay out flat on waxed paper.

While the lasagna is cooking, melt the butter and olive oil in a skillet. Sauté onion and garlic until golden. Remove from heat. Put chicken through food grinder. (If you do not have a grinder, all is not lost—use a fork and the same technique you'd use for tuna fish salad.) Combine chicken with onions, garlic, and the fat in which they were sautéed. Add egg, cream, and seasonings.

Cut each lasagna noodle into 2 or 3 pieces—each piece should be 3 to 4 inches long. Place a tablespoonful of the chicken filling on each piece and roll into tubular shape. Arrange next to one another, one layer deep, in a buttered baking dish. Set aside while you prepare the cheese sauce. Melt butter and thicken with flour. Add broth gradually, stirring constantly. Then add cream, salt, and pepper. Cook, stirring until thickened and smooth. Stir in ¾ cup grated Parmesan cheese. Remove sauce from heat and spoon over cannelloni in baking dish. Sprinkle with remaining cheese. Cover and refrigerate.

Before Serving

Preparation Time: 1 min.   *Cooking Time:* 10 min.

Preheat broiler. Place 4 to 5 inches from heat and broil for 10 min., or until sauce bubbles and top browns.   *Serves 6*

See also: Vegetable Soup with Meatballs (page 112), which makes an excellent main dish.

Top Secret

There comes a time in the life of every cook, when steaks, chops, and London Broil become the order of the day—either because there is absolutely no time the night before or just because the family likes them. Formulas for cooking a steak are almost as legion as recipes for "the only decent way" to mix a Martini. We think ours is the second-best way—nothing, of course can compete with charcoal broiling. The secret is soy sauce, and we title this "top secret" because we don't tell guests what we've done until after they've ooh-ed, aah-ed and gorged their way through the meat. People tend to think of soy sauce as a brown gook which appears on tables of Chinese restaurants, fit for nothing except sprinkling over chow mein. Since no one who really loves Chinese cooking eats chow mein anyway, soy sauce is considered a little declassé in some gourmet circles. Be that as it may, the fact remains that it not only flavors steaks or chops beautifully but, for reasons we don't pretend to understand, gives you the kind of crisp outside crust ordinarily obtainable only by charcoal grilling.

Here's the plot: if you have a spare 15 minutes before dinner, pour some soy sauce into a large platter or shallow roasting pan (not aluminum, please) and marinate the steaks or chops for 15 minutes, turning the meat occasionally. (If you crush a clove of garlic into the soy sauce, it won't do a bit of harm.) If you're short on time, just brush the soy sauce on both sides of the meat, using a pastry brush. Cook in an uncovered, ungreased skillet (375° if you're using an electric pan) until done. You can broil the meat if you prefer. We like the skillet because it's easier to clean and produces results that are just as good as the broiler.

It's a little difficult to give exact times for these dishes because the time will vary with the thickness of the meat and the exact point on the spectrum from rare to well done your family prefers for its meat. The following are suggested as a rough guide; test the meat by making a small cut in the center to see if it's done to your taste:

Steak: 4 to 5 min. on each side will give you a rare steak if it's about 1 inch thick.

Lamb Chops: 9 min. on each side

Veal Chops: 10 to 11 min. on each side

London Broil: 4 min. on each side (medium rare). Score the meat lightly on each side before marinating or brushing with the soy sauce. With the London Broil, try a can of mushroom gravy to which you have added ½ teaspoon minced garlic. Slice the meat by cutting at about a 45° angle.

Soy sauce also does lovely things to broiled chicken. Brush it over the chicken before broiling and don't add any other seasoning. Try brushing it over hamburgers, too.

Soy sauce can, incidentally, be used over again if you strain and refrigerate it between uses.

Section Two

ACCOMPANIMENTS

◆◆

◻ ## SALADS AND SALAD SUBSTITUTES ◻

There are those who will deny that there *is* any substitute for the mixed green salad. This chapter contains a few convincing arguments against that viewpoint. The Cucumber and Laban and the Vegetable Salad, for example, have been known to win high praise from some fairly ardent mixed green salad devotees. But, while you can win some concessions from the salad boys, you will have to include tossed salad in your repertoire and you may as well do it the easiest and best way.

Salad greens may, of course, be washed the night before and, if you don't have one of those marvelous wire salad baskets that hang over your faucet for drying greens, put this book face down on the table and go and buy one right away. We'll still be here when you get back. If you let your greens drip-dry in the salad basket for an hour or two while you're doing other things, you'll have a minimum of that tedious drying-with-paper-towels routine. Store your greens in a plastic bag in the refrigerator. Cucumbers, carrots, green peppers, radishes, etc., that you plan to include in the salad may be washed, pared, and chopped the night before and refrigerated in a separate plastic bag. You can't slice or quarter tomatoes ahead of time, but that problem has been solved by the fact that cherry tomatoes are now available most of the year. They can be washed the night before and added to the salad at the last minute. Since they do not need to be cut, there is no soggy tomato problem. The greens should be torn into the salad bowl just before serving. The other vegetables and the salad dressing can then be added.

If you have an electric blender, you can with little effort serve a different salad dressing each time even if you serve salad three or four times a week. If your blender is the kind which takes any Mason jar, it is a good idea to buy three or four small Mason jars and make three or four dressings at one time. If the dressing is then stored in the Mason jar, it can be put on the blender for a last minute reblending just before serving. You can start off with a basic French dressing and then divide it into parts, adding a different flavoring to each part—blue cheese or a few anchovies or some horseradish, parsley, garlic, herbs, onions, scallions, chili powder, or curry powder. If you want a gala twist, add some red caviar to your dressing after blending but before serving it.

Basic French Dressing

1 cup salad oil or olive oil (or a combination of the two)	1 teaspoon salt
	1 teaspoon dry mustard
¼ cup vinegar (wine or herb vinegar if you like)	½ teaspoon sugar
	Dash white pepper

The Night Before

Preparation Time: 5 min.

Put all ingredients in the blender container and blend until smooth—about 30 seconds. If you're making only one kind of dressing, your additional seasonings or herbs can be blended with the dressing. If you want to make more than one kind, add the appropriate seasonings to part of the dressing and reblend for a few sec. Refrigerate in a covered jar.

Before Serving
Preparation Time: ½ min.

Reblend for 10 seconds before serving.

Parsley Mayonnaise

1 egg
1 clove garlic, split
1½ cups parsley
½ teaspoon salt
½ teaspoon sugar
½ teaspoon mustard

⅛ teaspoon paprika
1 tablespoon vinegar
1 tablespoon lemon juice
Dash of Worcestershire sauce
¾ cup salad oil

The Night Before
Preparation Time: 5 min.

Put all ingredients except salad oil into a blender and blend at high speed for about 30 seconds. Switch to low speed, remove blender cover, and gradually add salad oil while the blender is running. When all the oil has been added, continue blending for a few seconds until mixture is smooth. Store in refrigerator in the blender container.

Before Serving
Preparation Time: 1 min.

Blend for a few seconds before transferring the mayonnaise to a serving dish. This is not only a good salad dressing but also makes an excellent sauce for fish.

Caesar Salad

Caesar Salad is usually a specialty of very high-priced, *haute-cuisine* restaurants. Actually, there's very little mystery to it and little work involved in preparing it; most of the preparation time given below is consumed in washing and drying the lettuce leaves. As a matter of fact, it's probably easier than most salad dressings—you needn't dice or chop anything; all you need to do is wield a set of measuring spoons. Caesar Salad's reputation for difficulty is probably due to the fact that it's a confusing thing to prepare at the last minute, but of course we've got *that* licked.

1 large head Romaine lettuce	⅛ teaspoon black pepper
3 tablespoons olive oil	¼ teaspoon salt
1 tablespoon lemon juice	⅛ teaspoon dry mustard
1 clove garlic, split	1 cup croutons
¼ cup grated Parmesan cheese	

. . . .

1 egg

The Night Before

Preparation Time: 12 min.

Wash and dry lettuce leaves and store whole leaves in plastic bag in refrigerator. Put olive oil, lemon juice, and split clove of garlic into a jar; cover jar, but do *not* refrigerate. Combine cheese, black pepper, dry mustard, and salt in a small dish or other container; cover and refrigerate. Put croutons into a small serving dish; cover—but don't refrigerate—dish.

Before Serving

Preparation Time: 4 min.

Note: If no one objects to the sight of raw egg, this is something that can be assembled easily and impressively at the table, as it is done in many restaurants. In that case, all you do in the kitchen is tear the lettuce.

Tear lettuce leaves into salad bowl. Sprinkle cheese mixture over lettuce. Shake jar of olive oil and lemon juice, remove garlic clove, and pour into salad bowl. Break raw egg into bowl and toss salad gently but thoroughly. Bring salad bowl and dish of croutons to the table (even if you are not assembling the whole salad at the table). Immediately before serving, add croutons and toss once more.   *Serves 4*

Cucumber and Laban Salad

2 cucumbers, finely diced   **1½ teaspoons salt**
2 cloves garlic   **1 tablespoon fresh or dried mint**

. . . .

¾ cup plain yogurt (laban)

The Night Before
Preparation Time: 13 min.

Cut the cucumbers into small dice and place in serving bowl. Place the salt on a wooden board or other firm surface and crush the garlic cloves directly into the salt, grinding them together with the back of a spoon. Sprinkle the garlic-salt mixture over the cucumbers. If using fresh mint, cut it fine and sprinkle it over the cucumbers. If you are using dried mint, crush it with the back of a spoon before adding it to the cucumbers. Toss the cucumbers and seasonings together, blending well. Cover and refrigerate the bowl.

Before Serving
Preparation Time: 1 min.

Add yogurt and toss the yogurt and cucumber mixture thoroughly before serving.   *Serves 4 to 5*

78

Endive Salad

4 endive stalks

. . . .

French dressing (with horseradish added, if you like)

The Night Before
Preparation Time: 3 min.

Wash and dry the endive, removing any discolored or bruised outer leaves. Refrigerate in a plastic bag.

Before Serving
Preparation Time: 2 min.

Place endive on a wooden chopping board and cut each stalk into 1-inch slices. The endive leaves will separate when you turn the slices into the salad bowl.

Endive and Beet Salad

4 endive stalks   1 small (8 oz.) can sliced beets

. . . .

French dressing or oil and vinegar in cruets to be passed at the table.

The Night Before
Preparation Time: 2 min.

Wash and dry the endive, removing any discolored or bruised outer leaves. Refrigerate the endive in a plastic bag. At the same time, put the can of beets in the refrigerator to chill.

Before Serving
Preparation Time: 3 min.

Cut endive into 1-inch slices and place in salad bowl. Add drained beets and toss lightly. The salad dressing may be

added before serving, or you can let everyone add his own
dressing from cruets of oil and vinegar at the table.   *Serves 4*

Spinach Salad with
Sour Cream Dressing

10-oz. package fresh spinach	¼ cup tarragon vinegar
2 or 3 cloves garlic	½ teaspoon salt
2 tablespoons salad oil	¼ teaspoon pepper
½ pint sour cream	

The Night Before
Preparation Time: 5 min.

Wash and dry spinach leaves. Tear into pieces and store
in a plastic bag in the refrigerator.

Place split garlic cloves and the salad oil in blender and
blend for 20 seconds. Add all remaining ingredients and run
blender until they are well mixed. Refrigerate in a covered jar.

Before Serving
Preparation Time: 1 min.

Put spinach in a salad bowl, add dressing and mix well.

Serves 4

Mike's Cole Slaw

This recipe is named for Mike Freeman, not because he
originated it, but because he loves it so much. And when
there's some of it in the refrigerator, it's really *his* cole slaw—
no one else gets more than a look at it. Brothers with huge
appetites notwithstanding, cole slaw must be prepared at least
one day, and preferably two, before it is to be eaten.

Incidentally, people who have eaten only the watery, sour-tasting kind of cole slaw commonly served in luncheonettes won't recognize the real thing, which is creamy and delicious.

2 lb. head green cabbage	3 tablespoons vinegar
2 carrots	⅓ cup sugar
1 green pepper	1½ cups Miracle Whip

The Night Before

Preparation Time: 15 min.

Wash and quarter cabbage, then shred it—a knife will shred it well enough, unless you insist on very finely shredded cabbage and want to use a shredder. Shred the carrots with a vegetable parer (or potato peeler). Mince the green pepper. Combine carrots and green pepper with cabbage. Mix vinegar, sugar, and Miracle Whip in an electric blender, or do it by hand, stirring vigorously.

Put half the cabbage mixture into a 2-quart casserole or bowl, then pour half of the dressing over it. Add remaining cabbage and dressing. It may look as though there isn't enough dressing for all that cabbage, but there is; it will drip down through the cabbage and, as it soaks, the cabbage will soften and lose about a third of its volume by yielding its moisture to the dressing. Cover casserole or bowl and refrigerate. Before you go to sleep, and again in the morning if you remember, stir the mixture with a spoon and then press it down with the back of the spoon.

Before Serving

Just check to make sure someone hasn't raided the refrigerator.   *Serves 6*

Vegetable Salad

There are some kitchen chores that are satisfying to the soul and some that are not. In the first category comes stirring things with a wooden spoon. In the second category, for one of us at least, is washing and tearing salad greens. If you share this antipathy, this recipe is heaven-sent. Even if you enjoy the tearin' of the green, you'll find this a pleasant change from ordinary salads.

1 small can sliced beets	¾ cup salad oil
1 small can string beans	¼ cup wine vinegar
1 small can whole carrots	1 teaspoon salt
1 medium onion, sliced	1 teaspoon sugar

(Actually, you can use any combination of vegetables that appeals to you. We try to avoid green peas because their color turns. Practically anything else is fine, though—corn, okra, lima beans—whatever your family likes or you happen to have on hand.)

The Night Before

Preparation Time: 5 min.

Drain the canned vegetables thoroughly. Place in a bowl with the sliced onion and cover with a marinade made of the oil, vinegar, salt, and sugar. Turn vegetables to coat well. Cover and refrigerate. Turn the vegetables again the next morning.

Before Serving

Preparation Time: 1 min.

Drain vegetables and serve. *Serves 4*

Gelatin Salads

Gelatin salads are what the sportswriters would call "a natural" for night-before preparation. It seems a little futile to give you lots of gelatin salad recipes since the gelatin manufacturers are more than eager to supply consumers with excellent collections of such recipes. Two basic recipes are given here for the primary purpose of indicating the time involved in preparation.

You can vary the vegetables included in your salad. We like combining a small amount of raw, chopped vegetables such as carrots, celery, or green pepper with some canned vegetables. (Try throwing a handful of canned julienne potato sticks in sometimes.) We prefer the gelatin to be a little tart, but you can, of course, vary the seasoning to produce a more bland or even a sharper base.

Incidentally, if the traditional method of unmolding a gelatin salad (dipping the mold in warm water and then running a knife around the edge) doesn't leave you too happy, here's a very safe method you can try. It was suggested by our friend, Marion Brown, whose cooking terminology seems to have taken on a slightly medical air, transmitted, no doubt, from her doctor-husband's office. (Marion is the only woman we know who makes a bouquet garni using medical gauze.) She describes this as "putting hot compresses on the mold." First run a knife around the edge of the mold to separate the gelatin from the sides of the mold. Put a plate over the top of the mold and invert the dishes. Then take a hot towel and press it over the top and sides of the mold. Wet the towel with hot water two or three times. Then place one hand on the bottom of the serving dish and one hand firmly on the top of the mold. Shake once, firmly, and you will find that your salad has unmolded without melting around the edges.

Basic Tomato Aspic

(This can be served either as a plain tomato aspic or with vegetables molded in it.)

1 envelope (1 tablespoon) un-
flavored gelatin
1¾ cups tomato juice
½ teaspoon celery salt
½ teaspoon sugar
3 tablespoons lemon juice

½ teaspoon Worcestershire
sauce
⅛ teaspoon Tabasco
1½ to 2 cups vegetables (optional)

83

The Night Before

Preparation Time: 5 to 7 min.

Pour ½ cup tomato juice into a saucepan. Sprinkle gelatin over juice. Heat over low flame, stirring, until gelatin is dissolved. Remove from heat and add remainder of tomato juice and seasonings. If you are making a plain tomato aspic, pour it into the mold, refrigerate, and forget it at this point.

If vegetables are to be added, refrigerate the gelatin mixture until it is slightly thickened. Then add vegetables, stir, and pour into mold. Refrigerate.

Before Serving

Preparation Time: 2 min.

Unmold salad and serve. You can, if you like, serve with salad dressing. Our preference is not to gild the lily. We admit, however, that a little mayonnaise, artistically applied, does dress up the salad.   *Serves 6*

Molded Beet Salad

1 envelope (1 tablespoon) un- flavored gelatin	½ teaspoon vinegar
	¼ cup lemon juice
1 can (1 lb.) julienne beets	¼ cup sugar
1½ teaspoons horseradish	½ cup celery, finely chopped

The Night Before

Preparation and Cooking Time: 10 min.

Mix gelatin, sugar, and ½ cup water in a saucepan. Heat, stirring, until gelatin is dissolved. Remove from heat. Pour juice from beets into a measuring cup and add enough water to make 1 cup of liquid. Add this liquid and the lemon juice, vinegar, and horseradish to the gelatin mixture. Refrigerate until mixture is slightly thickened; then add beets and celery. Stir well and pour into a mold. Refrigerate.

Preparation Time: 2 min.

Unmold salad and serve.   *Serves 6*

Cranberry-Orange Relish

½ lb. cranberries   1 teaspoon grated orange rind
1 cup sugar   ¼ cup water
¼ cup orange juice   ¼ cup slivered almonds

The Night Before

Preparation Time: 10 min.   *Cooking Time:* 10 to 12 min.

Put all ingredients, except almonds, in a saucepan. Cover and cook for 10 to 12 min. until cranberries burst. Strain juice off into another pan. Skim the froth off and return juice to cranberries. Add almonds, cool, and refrigerate.   *Serves 6*

Pickled Peppers

Red or green peppers (or a mix-   Oil
   ture of both)   Vinegar

The Night Before

Preparation Time: 5 min.   *Cooking Time:* 20 min.

Cut off and discard the tops of the peppers. Remove seeds and fibers from the peppers. Wash the peppers and place them in a pot with enough water to cover. Cook until tender— about 20 min. Drain and cool.

When peppers are cool, cut them into strips and put them into a jar. Combine oil and vinegar in equal amounts and pour the mixture over the peppers, being sure that there is enough liquid to cover the peppers. Cover the jar and refrigerate.

Before Serving

Preparation Time: ½ min.

Drain peppers and place in a serving dish.

Pickled Cucumbers

3 cucumbers, pared and thinly
    sliced
1 cup sugar

1⅓ cups vinegar
Scant ¼ teaspoon salt
⅛ teaspoon pepper

The Night Before

Preparation Time: 10 min.

Pare and slice cucumbers. Combine sugar, salt and pepper and dissolve in vinegar. Pour the mixture over the cucumbers and refrigerate.

Before Serving

Preparation Time: 1 min.

Drain cucumbers before serving.   *Serves 6*

See also: Three-Way Eggplant (page 101), which makes an excellent salad substitute.

☐ VEGETABLES ☐

Unless you are a vegetarian, you are not likely to want to spend as much time in the preparation of vegetables as you do on your main dish. For reasons of both health and taste, however, you do want your vegetables to have some variety and appeal. You will find included in this chapter several recipes using fresh vegetables, which take to night-before preparation (not all do), as well as some ideas for dressing up canned or frozen vegetables.

Hashed Brown Potatoes

4 medium potatoes
3 tablespoons grated onion

1¼ teaspoons salt
Dash of pepper

. . . .

3 tablespoons bacon fat or salad
   oil

3 tablespoons butter

The Night Before
Preparation Time: 13 min.   *Cooking Time:* 30 min.

Peel potatoes and cook in boiling water for 25 to 30 min. Chill and then grate potatoes and onion into a large bowl. Add salt and pepper, tossing very lightly. Cover and refrigerate.

Before Serving
Preparation Time: 5 min.   *Cooking Time:* 20 min.

If you're using an electric skillet, heat it to 300° before putting in the butter and bacon fat or salad oil. If you're using a nonelectric skillet, melt the fats in the skillet over a medium flame. When the fat bubbles, pour the potatoes into the pan and flatten them with a spatula. Shape the potatoes into a circle with the spatula, leaving a ¾-inch trough between the potatoes and the edge of the pan. Cook 20 min., then cut the potatoes from the edge of the pan to the center. Turn the two cut quarters over the uncut half and slide the whole thing onto a platter.   *Serves 4*

Baked Stuffed Potatoes

You can vary the seasonings when mashing the potatoes according to your whim, diet, or the contents of your refrigerator. Don't, however, omit brushing the potatoes with melted butter before storing. This keeps them moist.

4 baking potatoes, well scrubbed	2 teaspoons parsley, finely chopped
¾ cup sour cream	1 teaspoon salt
1 scallion, finely chopped	2 tablespoons melted butter

. . . .

¼ cup sour cream

The Night Before
Preparation Time: 15 min.   *Cooking Time:* 1 hr.

Bake potatoes in a 400° oven for 50 to 60 min., until soft. Allow to cool.

Cut a slice off the top of each potato. Scoop out the pulp and place in a mixing bowl. Add salt and sour cream and mash potatoes with an electric mixer or a potato masher. Stir in chopped scallion and parsley. Refill the potato shells with the mixture. Brush the potatoes on all sides with melted butter. Place in a baking dish, cover with waxed paper or aluminum foil and refrigerate.

Before Serving
Preparation Time: 1 min.   *Cooking Time:* 20 min.

Heat oven to 350°. Bake potatoes, uncovered, for 20 min. Before serving, put an additional dollop of sour cream on top of each potato or pass the sour cream separately.

Serves 4

Baked Wild Rice

3 tablespoons butter
1 green pepper, finely chopped
1 cup wild rice
1 teaspoon salt

2¾ cups canned chicken broth
(or half water, half chicken
broth)

The Night Before
Preparation and Cooking Time: 10 min.

Chop green pepper. Melt butter in saucepan and cook green pepper in the butter for 3 min., stirring occasionally. Meanwhile, grease the bottom and sides of a 2-quart casserole.

When green pepper has sautéed for 3 min., add the salt, rice, and chicken broth. Mix and turn into the greased casserole. Cover and refrigerate.

Before Serving
Preparation Time: 1 min.   *Cooking Time:* 1 hr.

Heat oven to 325°. Stir contents of casserole once, re-cover and place in oven. Bake for 1 hr.   *Serves 6*

Honeyed Carrots

1 bunch carrots
6 tablespoons honey

½ teaspoon salt
2 teaspoons lemon juice

. . . .

1 tablespoon flour

1 tablespoon melted butter

The Night Before
Preparation Time: 12 min.   *Cooking Time:* 1 hr.

Scrape the carrots and cut them into ¼-inch slices. Place in a saucepan with water to cover. Bring to a boil, then reduce heat and cook for 10 min. Add honey, lemon juice, and salt to liquid in pan; stir well. Cook slowly, uncovered, until liquid has been reduced by half. This will take about 45 to 50 min. Cool, cover, and refrigerate.

Before Serving

Preparation Time: 3 min.   *Cooking Time:* 6 min.

Start warming the carrots over a low flame. Meanwhile, melt the butter and blend the flour into it. Add the butter-flour mixture to the carrots. Cook, stirring occasionally, until the mixture comes to a boil. Cook for 1 min. more over a low flame.

Serves 4

Caesar Green Beans

1½ tablespoons salad oil or olive oil
1½ tablespoons wine vinegar

2 teaspoons minced onion
¼ teaspoon salt

. . . .

1 can (1 lb.) whole string beans
¾ cup croutons

3 tablespoons grated Parmesan cheese

The Night Before

Preparation Time: 5 min.

Mince onion and mix it with oil, vinegar, and salt. Store, covered, in refrigerator.

Before Serving

Preparation Time: 2 min.   *Cooking Time:* 5 min.

Drain beans and place in saucepan. Pour the oil-vinegar-onion mixture over beans. Add croutons. Stir well and cook until hot. Remove from heat and stir in Parmesan cheese.

Serves 4

Baked Beans

Canned baked beans can have the edge taken off their rather prosaic character by using the recipe for Baked Bean Casserole (page 63). If you are using this as a side dish, rather than as a main course, eliminate the meat and the orange.

Cut the rest of the ingredients in half and you will have an adequate serving for 4 people. The night-before preparation time will be reduced to about 6 min. and you can reduce the cooking time before serving to 30 min.

Italian Roasted Peppers

3 large green or red peppers
1 clove garlic
¼ bottle pine nuts
¼ cup pitted black olives, cut in pieces

½ cup flavored bread crumbs
¼ cup olive oil
½ teaspoon salt
⅛ teaspoon pepper

The Night Before

Preparation Time: 10 min.   *Cooking Time:* 35 to 40 min.

Heat oven to 350°. Cut peppers in strips, removing seeds, and place in shallow baking pan. Add chopped garlic, nuts, olives, salt, and pepper and mix. Sprinkle bread crumbs over mixture and pour oil over top. Bake, uncovered, at 350°, for 35 to 40 min., stirring occasionally. Store in refrigerator.

Before Serving

Preparation Time: 1 min.   *Cooking Time:* 5 to 10 min.

The peppers can be reheated either in the oven at 300° for 10 min. or in a saucepan on top of the stove for about 5 min.

Serves 6

Baked Stuffed Mushrooms

1 lb. fresh mushrooms
3 tablespoons butter
1 tablespoon minced parsley
1 egg, lightly beaten

⅓ cup seasoned bread crumbs
1½ tablespoons butter (for dotting)

The Night Before
Preparation and Cooking Time: 10 min.

Wash and dry mushrooms. Remove stems and chop them. Sauté stems in butter for 4 or 5 min. Remove from heat, add parsley, egg, and bread crumbs. Toss until well mixed. Spoon some of this mixture into the hollow of each mushroom cap. Place mushrooms in a shallow, lightly buttered baking dish. Dot with butter, cover, and refrigerate.

Before Serving

Cooking Time: 20 min.

Place uncovered baking dish in a cold oven. Set heat control at 350° and bake for 20 min.

Serves 4

Vegetable Potpourri

We tend to use this as a company dish—first, because it enables you to use fresh vegetables in an unusual and delicious stew that does not need to be prepared just before serving and, second, because we've never been able to figure out what you'd do with the other half of the eggplant if you tried cutting the recipe in half.

¼ cup olive oil
3 cloves garlic, chopped
1 large onion, sliced
2 zucchini, pared and sliced
1 small eggplant, peeled and cubed

2 green peppers, cut in 2-inch chunks
4 tomatoes, cut in eighths
¼ cup water
3 tablespoons flour

. . . .

2 teaspoons salt
¼ teaspoon pepper

2 tablespoons capers

The Night Before

Preparation Time: 22 min.   *Cooking Time:* 1 hr., 15 min.

Heat the olive oil in a large, heavy pan. Sauté the garlic and onion, over low heat, until yellow but not crisp. While this is cooking, pare and slice the zucchini, peel and cube the eggplant, wash, seed, and cut the green peppers in cubes. Put these vegetables in a bag with the flour and shake well until the pieces are lightly coated with flour. When the onion is yellow, add the eggplant, zucchini, peppers, and the ¼ cup water. Stir well, cover, and cook over low flame for 1 hr.

Wash the tomatoes and cut them in eighths. After the vegetables have cooked for an hour, add the tomatoes and stir well. Cook 15 min. longer, then remove from heat, cool slightly, and refrigerate.

Before Serving

Preparation Time: 3 min.   *Cooking Time:* 15 min.

Add the salt, pepper, and capers. Simmer, uncovered, for 15 min., stirring occasionally.   *Serves 8*

Eggplant Casserole

1 medium eggplant	3 tablespoons flour
2 cups canned tomatoes	1½ teaspoons salt
1 green pepper	1 tablespoon brown sugar
1 medium onion	Bread crumbs
3 tablespoons butter	Grated cheese

The Night Before
Preparation and Cooking Time: 25 min.

Peel and dice the eggplant. Cook for 10 min. in boiling water. While it is cooking, chop the tomatoes, onion, and pepper.

Melt the butter and add the flour, stirring. Add the tomatoes, pepper, onion, salt, and sugar. Cook for 5 min.

Drain the eggplant and place it in a greased 1-quart casserole. Top with vegetable mixture. Cover lightly with bread crumbs and sprinkle with grated cheese. Cover and refrigerate.

Before Serving

Preparation Time: 1 min.   *Cooking Time:* 35 min.

Bake, uncovered, in 350° oven for 35 min.   *Serves 5 to 6*

See also: Three-Way Eggplant (page 101).

Baked Spiced Fruit (Sugar and Spice and Nice with Pork or Lamb)

4 canned peach halves
4 canned pear halves
4 canned pineapple slices
6 maraschino cherries

3 tablespoons butter
6 tablespoons light brown sugar
1 teaspoon curry powder

The Night Before

Preparation Time: 10 min.   *Cooking Time:* 1 hr.

Preheat oven to 325°. Drain peaches, pears, pineapple, and cherries, then wipe thoroughly dry. Melt butter in small saucepan. Remove from heat and add sugar and curry powder. Place fruit in small baking dish, spoon sauce over fruit. Bake, uncovered, for 1 hr. Cover and refrigerate.

Before Serving

Cooking Time: 30 min.

Preheat oven to 325°. Take cover off dish and bake for 30 min. Remove from oven, re-cover dish and let stand for 5 min. before serving.   *Serves 4 to 6*

Zucchini Casserole

2 tablespoons butter
4 to 5 small zucchini (about 3
    cups when sliced)

2 medium onions, sliced
1 can (1 lb.) stewed tomatoes

• • • • • • • • • • • • •

Grated cheese

The Night Before
Preparation and Cooking Time: 15 min.

Sauté the sliced onions in the melted butter until golden. Meanwhile, pare and slice the zucchini. Remove onions from stove, stir in sliced zucchini and stewed tomatoes. Cover and refrigerate.

Before Serving
Preparation Time: 1 min.   *Cooking Time:* 45 min.

Heat oven to 350°. Sprinkle grated cheese liberally over top of casserole, completely covering the other ingredients. Bake, uncovered, for 45 min.   *Serves 5 to 6*

Sorcery and Saucery (How to Hide Behind a Can of Peas)

No one but a gourmet society demands that every course in a meal be a special and elaborate one, and if you have a good main course, you can get by with frozen or canned vegetables. There are times, though, when it's nice to have a few tricks up your can opener—for the sake of variety, or taste, or eye-appeal, or deceiving dinner guests.

The range of special effects to be achieved is almost unlimited—it would be hopeless to attempt to list all of them. We have included just four recipes for sauces, some suggestions for toppings, and a few specific ideas. Those which cannot be prepared the night before take no more than 3 or 4 min. of preparation time before serving.

Any of the following toppings will give canned or frozen vegetables a touch of distinction.

Buttered Crumbs: Mix equal amounts of melted butter and dry bread crumbs. Use to top vegetable casseroles or mix with cooked vegetables.

95

Crumbled Hard-Cooked Egg: Sprinkle over asparagus and other bright green vegetables.

Crumbled Bacon: Goes well with almost any vegetable, except beets.

Sautéed Onions and/or Sautéed Mushrooms: Use to mix with any vegetable. (The onions and mushrooms alone are a delicious vegetable dish.)

SAUCERY

While only one of these sauces lends itself to night-before preparation, the others can be prepared so quickly that you won't mind doing them just before serving.

Butter and Almond Sauce
(for almost all green vegetables, rice)

1 stick (½ cup) butter
¼ cup sliced or slivered almonds

1 tablespoon lemon juice (optional)

Sauté almonds in butter until golden brown. Stir in lemon juice.

Chive-Lemon Butter Sauce
(for artichokes, asparagus, broccoli, Brussels sprouts)

1 stick (½ cup) butter
¼ cup lemon juice

2 tablespoons fresh or frozen chives, minced

Place all ingredients in small saucepan and cook over low heat until butter is melted.

Swiss or Parmesan Cheese Sauce—
can be made the night before and reheated
(for green vegetables, onions, tomatoes, pasta)

1 tablespoon butter
1 tablespoon flour
½ cup chicken broth
¼ cup heavy cream or evaporated milk

¼ cup grated Swiss or Parmesan cheese

Melt butter, stir in flour, and cook until thickened. Gradually add broth, stirring constantly, then add cream. Cook, stirring, until thickened and smooth, then stir in grated cheese.

Blender Hollandaise Sauce
(*for asparagus, broccoli, cauliflower*)

1 egg yolk	4 tablespoons (½ stick) melted
⅛ teaspoon salt	butter
1½ teaspoons lemon juice	Dash of paprika

Blend egg yolk and salt for just an instant, then add other ingredients. Blend until sauce is thick and perfectly smooth. Heat in top of double boiler, being careful not to let sauce get so hot that it curdles.

SORCERY

Parsley Potatoes: Gently cook canned tiny, whole potatoes in a mixture of melted butter and chopped parsley until potatoes are heated through and well coated with parsley butter. For each medium-sized can of potatoes, use 4 tablespoons (½ stick) butter and 2 tablespoons parsley.

Oregano Potatoes: Sauté canned tiny, whole potatoes in melted butter and oregano. Cook over medium heat until potatoes are golden brown and slightly crisp. For each large-sized can of potatoes, use ½ cup (1 stick) butter and 1 or more tablespoons oregano, to taste.

Creamed Corn (Canned) or Creamed Spinach (Frozen) Casserole: The night before, place corn or cooked creamed spinach in a buttered casserole dish. Top with buttered crumbs. Before serving, bake at 350° until vegetables are heated and crumbs are golden brown—about 10 to 15 min.

Peas and Cocktail Onions: Heat canned peas, or cook frozen peas, and drain. Mix with cocktail onions (they come in a jar). Dress with butter and serve, or mix with sour cream, as follows: Return drained peas and onions to saucepan, add sour cream (¼ cup for each 10 oz. package of frozen peas), and cook just until sour cream is heated through—don't let it cook long enough for the sour cream to curdle.

Green Beans and Mushrooms: Using the same procedure as above (peas and onions) combine green beans and canned sliced mushrooms with either butter or sour cream.

Cauliflower, Broccoli, or Brussels Sprouts au Gratin: The night before, cook frozen vegetables just until you can pierce them with a fork—they should still be quite firm. Turn into a greased casserole dish. Prepare Swiss or Parmesan Cheese Sauce (page 96). Before serving, pour sauce over vegetables, top with buttered crumbs, and bake at 350° for 15 min.

□ BREAD □

The easiest, and possibly the most elegant, way of casting bread upon the table is to purchase flaky croissants from a good French bakery. But if you are fresh out of either a good French bakery or a large food budget, or if you served croissants to these people *last* time they came to dinner, there are some easy and very impressive alternatives. All the work, except for heating or brown-and-serving, is done the night before, of course. None of the following requires more than 5 or 10 minutes of night-before preparation time.

GROUP I—USING BROWN-AND-SERVE FRENCH BREAD OR ROLLS

Split, but do not separate, bread or rolls through the middle and spread each half with any one of the following. Then close into original shape, wrap securely with foil or plastic wrap, and refrigerate. Before serving, brown according to package directions.

Parsley Bread

1 stick (¼ lb.) butter   ¼ cup chopped scallions
¼ cup chopped parsley

Cream softened butter with parsley and scallions. (This can be done in the blender, too, eliminating the necessity for chopping the vegetables.) Spread on bread.

Garlic and Parmesan Bread

1 stick (¼ lb.) butter   Grated Parmesan cheese
2 cloves garlic, crushed

Cream softened butter with crushed garlic. Spread on bread; sprinkle Parmesan cheese on each half.

Anchovy Bread

1 stick (¼ lb.) butter   **1 tablespoon anchovy paste**

Cream softened butter with anchovy paste. Spread on bread.

GROUP II—USING FULLY BAKED BREAD OR ROLLS

Cut French bread into rounds, or split rolls through the middle. Spread with any one of the mixtures suggested above; or spread with softened butter, then top each round with one of the following:

> Dried oregano
> Cinnamon and sugar
> Chopped olives
> Minced green pepper
> Rolled anchovy filet

Place rounds in a baking dish or on a cookie sheet, cover with foil or waxed paper, and refrigerate. Before serving, heat in oven at 350° for about 10 min. (A special, but not absolutely necessary, touch when using cinnamon and sugar is to run it under the broiler for the last minute or two.) Serve hot.

Even though it cannot be prepared or assembled the night before, we just can't resist telling you about fried garlic bread. If you like your garlic bread both crunchy and moist, and literally dripping with garlic, try this: sauté lots of minced or crushed garlic in lots of butter, dip both sides of rounds of French bread or slices of white bread in the melted garlic butter so that the bread soaks up all the butter, then fry over fairly high heat until both sides are crisp and lightly browned.

Section Three

ACCESSORIES BEFORE AND AFTER THE FACT

❖❖❖❖❖❖❖❖❖❖❖❖❖❖❖❖❖❖❖❖❖❖❖❖❖❖❖❖❖❖❖❖❖❖❖❖

☐ APPETIZERS AND SOUPS ☐

Three-Way Eggplant

This dish acquired its name because it has at various times appeared on our tables serving three different functions. It is an excellent canapé spread on tiny slices of rye bread or dark pumpernickel. Or it can appear as a scoop of eggplant on a lettuce leaf as a first course. Last, but not least, it can be served as an excellent cold vegetable for a night when you don't want to be bothered making a salad. It can be made at any convenient time and kept in the refrigerator for a week—provided that you lock the refrigerator.

1 medium eggplant	1½ teaspoons salt
¼ cup minced onion	1 teaspoon sugar
2 tablespoons olive oil	⅛ teaspoon pepper
¼ cup lemon juice	

The Night Before

Preparation Time: 15 min.   *Cooking Time:* 15 min.

Heat oven to 475°. While it is heating, squeeze lemons and chop onion. Bake eggplant for about 15 min. or until skin turns dark brown. Cool and peel.

If you have a blender, blend cubes of eggplant together

with rest of ingredients. If you have no blender, chop the eggplant fine and then stir in other ingredients. Refrigerate.

Before Serving
Preparation Time: 1 min.

Pour off any excess liquid and serve.

Serves 5 to 6 as an appetizer or vegetable
Serves 12 to 20 as an hors d'oeuvre

Shrimp Toast

½ lb. raw shrimp, shelled and deveined
½ medium onion
⅛ teaspoon ground ginger
½ teaspoon salt

Dash of black pepper
1 egg white
6 slices white bread, stale or dried in oven
½ cup fine dry bread crumbs

. . . .

½ cup salad oil

The Night Before
Preparation Time: 15 min.

(*Note:* It is assumed that the shrimp have been shelled and deveined at the fish market.)

Put onions and shrimp through food grinder, using medium blade. If you do not have a food grinder, mince them with a sharp knife. Add ginger, salt, and pepper. Beat egg white lightly with a fork, then combine it with the shrimp mixture.

Remove crusts from slices of bread and cut each slice diagonally so that you have two triangles. Spread shrimp mixture on bread triangles. Heap bread crumbs on top, gently patting them down with your hands. Place on a large platter, cover with aluminum foil, and refrigerate.

Before Serving
Preparation and Cooking Time: 4 min.

Heat oil until very hot (400° in an electric skillet) and fry shrimp toast for 1 min. on each side. Drain on paper towels and serve.

Serves 6

Dip de Luxe: Caviar and Sour Cream

While not wishing to offend the sensibilities of those caviar aficionados who feel that only the twelve-dollars-per-pound stuff is worth eating, we contend that for this particular purpose the least expensive jar of caviar on your supermarket shelf will serve very well. It's the *blending* of flavors and textures that's important here, not the outrageously fine quality of one ingredient. The governing rule: anything that costs two bits a taste ought to be really tasted. Don't mask its flavor by combining it with sour cream, wine, or even with dinner, for that matter.

2 cups (1 pint) sour cream
4 to 6 oz. red caviar or red and black mixed (the exact quantity depends on how salty you like your dip.)

3 to 4 tablespoons finely minced onion

The Night Before

Preparation Time: 5 min.

Add caviar and onion to sour cream. (You can do this right in the sour cream container if you wish.) Mix well and turn into serving dish. Refrigerate until ready to serve.

Warning: Since this dip takes so little time to prepare, you may be tempted to wait until just before serving time to put it together. Don't—it takes at least 6 to 8 hrs. for the flavors to blend properly.   *Serves 8 to 10*

Guacamole Nassau

We wish we could say, in the airy tone that so many cook book authors use, that "we first tasted this lovely avocado salad in a quaint little restaurant on the island of Nassau, in the Bahamas." In the first place, we've never been to the

Bahamas. Furthermore, Guacamole is a Mexican dish. (We've never been *there*, either.) All this by way of acknowledging the contributor of this recipe, Mrs. Chloe Nassau, who lives on the exotic island of Manhattan, in New York.

2 large ripe avocados
1 green pepper, finely chopped
1 tomato, peeled and finely chopped
3 tablespoons grated onion
1 teaspoon olive oil

2 teaspoons lime juice
1½ teaspoons chili powder
¼ teaspoon salt, plus more to taste
⅛ teaspoon black pepper
Mayonnaise

The Night Before

Preparation Time: 11 min.

Peel and chop tomato. (Tomato can be peeled easily if you first put it on the end of a fork and rotate directly in the open burner flame until the skin blisters. Then hold under cold running water and peel.) Seed and chop green pepper. Grate onion. Set aside.

Mash avocados (they *must* be ripe) and immediately add lime juice. Add vegetables and all other ingredients except mayonnaise. Taste and add more salt and/or pepper, according to taste. Place in a jar or other deep container that is about 3 or 4 inches in diameter. Cover surface with a thick layer of mayonnaise—this will prevent discoloration. Cover container securely with its own tight-fitting cover or with plastic wrap and a rubber band (just in case).

Before Serving

Preparation Time: 1 min.

Mix mayonnaise into the Guacamole. Serve as a first course or salad by piling on lettuce leaves arranged on individual plates; or serve as a dip to accompany pre-dinner cocktails by heaping into a bowl and surrounding with potato or corn chips.

Serves 4 as a salad or first course
Serves 8 to 10 as a dip

Mushroom Biscuits

1 cup (about ⅓ pound) fresh mushrooms, thinly sliced
10 ready-to-bake frozen biscuits
3 tablespoons butter

1½ tablespoons flour
¼ cup milk
¼ cup chicken bouillon
⅛ teaspoon salt

The Night Before

Preparation and Cooking Time: 14 min.

Clean and slice mushrooms. Melt 1 tablespoon butter in a small saucepan; melt the other 2 tablespoons butter in a small skillet. Place mushrooms in skillet and cook over low flame until they are soft and begin to turn brown. Stir flour into melted butter in saucepan and cook butter and flour together, stirring, for about 30 seconds. Take off heat, add milk, bouillon, and salt, stirring as you add them. Cook over medium heat, stirring constantly, until mixture is thickened and smooth. Remove from heat and add sautéed mushrooms. Let cool slightly while you prepare the biscuits.

Cut a well in the top of each frozen biscuit. A curved grapefruit knife does this very easily. (The biscuits should not be thawed at this point.) Spoon slightly cooled mushroom mixture into each well. Place biscuits on cookie sheet, cover with foil and refrigerate (do not freeze).

Before Serving

Preparation Time: ½ min.   *Cooking Time: 7 to 9 min.*

Preheat oven to temperature specified on biscuit package (usually 450° or 475°). Place biscuits, still on cookie sheet, in oven and bake for length of time directed on package (usually about 7 min.).   *Serves 4 to 6*

Antipasto

The Italian Antipasto is no dainty little affair—it has a large quantity and variety of ingredients, including meat, fish, and vegetables. Although it is commonly served as the first course of a meal featuring pasta (Antipasto means "before the pasta"), this is something to keep in mind when building a meal around main-dish soups.

The night before, arrange the Antipasto either on one large platter or on individual salad plates. Starting with a bed of lettuce leaves or watercress, use any appealing or convenient combination of the ingredients listed below. Cover tightly with plastic wrap or foil before refrigerating. Serve with cruets of wine vinegar and olive oil and let each person add his own dressing.

Prosciutto (Italian ham)
Genoa salami
Anchovies
Tuna fish—packed in olive oil
Pimentos
Green or red peppers (Pickled Peppers, page 85, are very good)
Green and black olives
Cucumbers
Radishes
Cherry tomatoes
Shrimp
Capers
Slices of red onion
Sardines

Mozzarella Appetizer

10 thin slices white bread
¼ lb. mozzarella cheese, very thinly sliced

1 small can anchovy filets
1 teaspoon dried oregano

The Night Before

Preparation Time: 4 min.

Toast bread slices very lightly, then trim crusts and cut each slice into trangles, rectangles, or rounds—depending on what strikes your fancy and suits the shape of your cheese. On each piece, place a slice of cheese, an anchovy, and a few flakes of oregano. Place on broiler tray, cover with plastic wrap or foil, and refrigerate.

Before Serving

Preparation Time: ½ min.   *Cooking Time:* 2 min.

Remove broiler tray from refrigerator, uncover, and broil mozzarella appetizers until cheese melts—about 2 min.

Serves 6 to 8

Marinated Shrimp

2 lbs. shelled, deveined shrimp
¾ cup olive oil
2 onions, diced
3 split cloves garlic
2 large onions, sliced in thin rings

½ teaspoon chili powder
¼ teaspoon dry mustard
1½ teaspoons salt
½ teaspoon black pepper
½ cup vinegar

The Night Before

Preparation and Cooking Time: 25 min.

Sauté the chopped onions and garlic in ¼ cup olive oil for 10 min. Add the shrimp and sauté for 7 or 8 min., stirring a few times during cooking. Remove shrimp from pan with a slotted spoon and set aside to cool while you prepare sauce.

Mix the remaining ½ cup olive oil together with all the other ingredients listed. Add the shrimp, being sure to coat all the shrimp with the marinade. Cover the dish and refrigerate. Whenever you go to the refrigerator, take a spoon with you and baste the shrimp.

This dish should be served cold. *Serves 8 as an appetizer*
Serves up to 25 as an hors d'oeuvre

Seafood Cocktails

If you are fortunate enough to live in the vicinity of a good fish market, don't overlook the possibilities of clams or oysters on the half-shell as an elegant first course. Don't be intimidated by the fact that restaurants ordinarily serve these on a bed of crushed ice or in serving dishes obviously designed for this purpose alone. If your clams or oysters are being taken directly from the refrigerator, the crushed ice is more decorative than necessary. You can use ordinary dinner or service plates covered with a paper doily. Sprigs of parsley between the shells are enough to relieve the barren look. Use a small glass custard cup in the center of each plate to hold the cocktail sauce.

This sauce can be used not only for clams and oysters, but for shrimp, lobster, and crabmeat cocktails as well.

¾ cup ketchup
¼ cup mayonnaise

1 tablespoon horseradish
1 tablespoon lemon juice

The Night Before

Preparation Time: 2 min.

Mix all ingredients in blender or by hand. Taste and, if desired, add another teaspoon of horseradish.

Makes 1 cup sauce

Chopped Liver

1 lb. beef (or calf or chicken) liver
2 medium onions
2 eggs, hard boiled

6 tablespoons chicken fat or mayonnaise
1 teaspoon salt
⅛ teaspoon pepper

The Night Before

Preparation Time: 15 min.   *Cooking Time:* 10 to 12 min.

Cut liver into 2- to 3-inch chunks. Place in pot with water to cover and cook until centers of liver chunks are no longer pink—this will take 10 to 12 min. While the liver is cooking, hard-boil 2 eggs and peel the onions and cut them in chunks.

Put liver, onions, and eggs through the fine blade of your food grinder. If you are using chicken fat, melt it in a small skillet before adding it to the liver. Add the chicken fat or mayonnaise and the salt and pepper to the liver mixture and mix well.

Before Serving

Preparation Time: 3 min.

To serve as an appetizer, for each portion put a mound of chopped liver on a couple of lettuce leaves and garnish with a sprig of parsley. This can also be served with crackers as a cocktail spread.

Serves 6 as an appetizer
Serves 12 as a cocktail spread

Cheese Ball

4 oz. Roquefort cheese
8 oz. Cheddar cheese, grated or shredded
6 oz. (2 small packages) cream cheese
1 onion, finely minced

1 teaspoon Worcestershire sauce
½ cup chopped walnuts
3 tablespoons chopped chives or parsley (optional)

The Night Before

Preparation Time: 12 min.

Allow the cheeses to stand at room temperature until they soften. Combine them with onion and Worcestershire. Refrigerate for about an hour, until firm enough to mold into a ball. Roll the cheese ball in chopped walnuts and, if you

109

wish, chopped chives or parsley. Wrap in waxed paper and refrigerate.

Before Serving

Let stand at room temperature for 10 min. Serve with crackers or dark bread. The uneaten portion of the cheese ball is easily salvaged: mold it back into a ball, reroll in chopped walnuts, wrap, and freeze. It will keep beautifully in the freezer.   *Serves 8*

Chicken Egg Drop Soup

2 scallions (green onions), with their green tops, chopped

. . . .

4 cups chicken broth (or 2 cans [14 oz.] uncondensed chicken soup or 2 cans of condensed chicken soup plus one can of water)
1½ tablespoons cornstarch

¼ teaspoon sugar
½ teaspoon salt
⅛ teaspoon pepper
1 egg, beaten
¼ cup cold water

The Night Before

Preparation Time: 2 min.

Wash and chop scallions and store in refrigerator in waxed paper or plastic bag.

Before Serving

Preparation Time: 3 min.   *Cooking Time:* 7 min.

Heat broth to boiling point. Meanwhile, beat the egg in one small dish or glass. In another, make a smooth paste of the cornstarch and cold water; then add the sugar, salt, and pepper to the cornstarch mixture.

When the soup has boiled, pour the cornstarch mixture slowly into it, stirring constantly. Allow the soup to reach the boiling point again. Cook and stir for 1 min. until soup is thick and translucent. Then add the beaten egg, very slowly, stirring constantly. When all the egg has been added, remove the soup from the stove, pour into tureen or serving dish and sprinkle scallions over top.   *Serves 4*

Chicken Soup with Matzo Balls (Knaidlach)

3 eggs

1 to 2 teaspoons salt (sorry, the two of us don't agree on the amount; you'll have to make up your own mind)

Dash of pepper

½ cup matzo meal

1 tablespoon melted **chicken fat** or butter

. . . .

4 cups chicken soup (or 2 cans [14 oz.] uncondensed chicken soup or 2 cans condensed chicken soup plus one can water)

The Night Before

Preparation Time: 8 min.

Separate eggs. Beat whites until stiff. In a separate bowl, beat the yolks until they are light. Add to the yolks the melted chicken fat or butter, salt, and pepper. Fold the yolk mixture into the egg whites. Then fold in the matzo meal, a spoonful at a time. Refrigerate this batter for at least 1 hr. Then form the mixture into 12 balls. Cover with waxed paper and refrigerate overnight.

Before Serving

Preparation Time: 2 min.   *Cooking Time:* 35 min.

Boil 2 quarts water in a fairly wide saucepan. Drop the matzo balls gently into boiling water, reduce heat and simmer slowly, covered, for 30 min. The chicken soup can be heated in a separate pot during the last part of this cooking period. When matzo balls are cooked, remove with a slotted spoon and place in soup.

(If you have enough chicken soup to be able to spare some, cook the matzo balls directly in the pot of soup. You'll lose a fair amount of soup through absorption, so be sure you have enough to start with.) *Serves 4*

Vegetable Soup

This is a very hearty—and delicious—soup. If you're planning to use it as the main course, make it with the meat balls. If you plan it as the first but not the main course of a meal, omit the meat balls.

6 cups canned beef broth
1 can (1 lb.) Italian tomatoes
3 stalks celery, with leaves
1 carrot

1 teaspoon oregano
½ cup small pasta or noodle
   flakes

FOR MEAT BALLS

2 slices toast
1 lb. chopped chuck
1 egg

1 clove garlic
1 teaspoon salt
3 tablespoons butter

. . . .

Grated Parmesan cheese

The Night Before
Preparation Time: 12 min. for soup only or 30 min. with meat balls
Cooking Time: 25 min.

If you have an electric blender, peel and coarsely cube the carrot and cut the celery in chunks. Blend, using the canned tomatoes and some of the beef broth as your liquid in the blending process. Pour all the beef broth and the blended vegetables, tomatoes, and oregano into a pot and bring to a boil. Then cover and simmer for 10 min.:

OR
If you have no blender, bring the beef broth to a boil while you chop the peeled carrot and the celery into fine pieces.

When the broth is boiling add the canned tomatoes, celery, carrot, and oregano and simmer, covered, for 12 min.

Add the pasta or noodle flakes and simmer for an additional 10 min. Cover and refrigerate.

MEAT BALLS

Soak the toast in water and squeeze dry. Toss lightly with the beef, beaten egg, chopped garlic, and salt. Shape into small meat balls, one inch in diameter. Brown the meat balls in butter while the soup is cooking. Refrigerate separately in a covered bowl.

Before Serving

Preparation Time: 1 min.   *Cooking Time:* 10 min.

Add meat balls to soup and simmer for 10 min. until hot. Serve with grated Parmesan cheese.   *Serves 6*

See also: Cabbage Soup (page 64).

☐ DESSERTS ☐

Dessert is the easiest course of all to fit into the night-before approach to cooking. Almost any dessert—with the exception of things like soufflés and crepes—can be prepared in advance without benefit of special techniques or recipes. For that reason, we have not attempted to provide an exhaustive chapter on desserts.

Cake mixes and ready-to-bake pie shells are two boons to the working person. They enable you to skip the steps that consume time (and which give you a plethora of bowls and utensils to wash) and concentrate on imaginative fillings and decoration. Unless you're a champion baker, the results you get with a cake mix will probably be nearly as good as those you would get if you were baking your cake from scratch.

Although the night-before cook has an almost unlimited choice of desserts, the time and effort for their preparation varies considerably. You can make an instant chocolate pudding with cold milk, which takes a few seconds, or a four-layer cake made with four different kinds of cake and three different fillings, which takes all night. The few dessert recipes we have chosen for inclusion in this book were selected because they are slightly unusual and produce interesting results for the little time and trouble they take.

While we think you'll enjoy these desserts, we must admit that when we're short of time we find dessert the easiest course on which to save time and effort. Truth to tell, it is hard to find a dessert more satisfying than fresh fruit in season and a well chosen cheese. If you want something sweeter and less sophisticated, you can't go wrong with ice cream, particularly if you keep on hand an assortment of toppings. There are now a number of really good frozen cakes and pastries available and a few packages of these tucked into your freezer are good insurance for the nights when you're tired or unambitious. At the risk of destroying your image of our pampered families, we must admit that we use the simplest desserts unless we're having company. For the nights when you want to show off a little, these desserts will achieve the desired end.

Preparing desserts the night before does entail more risk than other dishes. Oh, your dessert won't lose any flavor overnight, and its texture and appearance won't suffer an iota; it will be as tempting as ever. It will be too tempting, in fact, and the kids will have eaten it after school. For this problem, we offer no solution.

Biscuit Tortoni

1 cup heavy cream
Scant ⅓ cup confectioner's
   (powdered) sugar

1 egg white
½ cup macaroon crumbs
1 to 1½ teaspoons cream sherry

The Night Before

Preparation Time: 15 min.

Prepare macaroon crumbs (the electric blender does this beautifully—and quickly!). Whip the cream. Fold in sugar, a tablespoonful at a time. Beat egg white until stiff. Using about a third of each at a time, fold the following into the whipped cream: the beaten egg white, ⅓ of the cup macaroon crumbs, and the sherry.

Spoon the mixture into paper muffin cups. Sprinkle the tops with remaining macaroon crumbs. Place in freezer, uncovered, until quite firm, then wrap in plastic bag and return to freezer.

Serves 6

Pound Cake Pudding

It's difficult to describe this dessert, which is somewhere between a pudding-like cake and a cake-like pudding. Although it is moist enough to be served as is, we like it best with the light custard sauce given below. Whipped cream (from a time-saving pressure can) also makes a nice topping for this pudding.

2 cups pound cake crumbs, stale or toasted	4 tablespoons butter, melted
¾ cup milk	4 tablespoons sugar
2 eggs, beaten	1 tablespoon lemon juice
1 cup pineapple preserves	¼ teaspoon vanilla
	Pinch of salt

LIGHT CUSTARD SAUCE

1 egg yolk, lightly beaten	¼ teaspoon vanilla
½ cup milk	Pinch of salt
1½ tablespoons sugar	

The Night Before

Preparation Time: Pudding, 5 min.; Custard Sauce, 7 min.

Cooking Time: 50 min. to 1 hr.

PUDDING

Preheat oven to 350°. Put cake crumbs in a bowl, pour milk over them, and soak for 10 or 12 min. (If you are going to use the light custard sauce, prepare it while the cake crumbs are soaking.) Mix all other ingredients for the pudding together in a separate bowl. Add this mixture to the soaked crumbs and blend very well. Butter a 1-quart baking dish, preferably a loaf-shaped one, and transfer the mixture into the baking dish. Bake at 350° for 50 to 60 min. (check after 50 min. and bake longer if necessary), until appearance of pudding resembles a cake that is beginning to get a golden brown color. Let cool and refrigerate.

LIGHT CUSTARD SAUCE

Put all ingredients into the top of a double boiler and cook over boiling water, stirring constantly, until the sauce is slightly thickened—the consistency should be halfway between liquid and custard. This will take about 5 min. Pour into a sauce boat or small serving dish and refrigerate.

Before Serving

Preparation Time: 1 min.

Slice the pudding and arrange on a platter or on individual dessert dishes. If you are using whipped cream as a topping, add it before serving. If you are using the light custard sauce, pass it in a sauce boat or serving dish.   *Serves 6*

Cheese Pudding

1 lb. pot cheese, Hoop cheese, or uncreamed cottage cheese
½ cup granulated sugar
1 cup white raisins

½ pint sour cream
½ lemon
3 eggs
1½ cups cornflakes (slightly crushed)

. . . .

3 to 4 tablespoons brown sugar

The Night Before

Preparation Time: 15 min.

Mix all ingredients except the cornflakes and brown sugar together, using the juice from the half lemon as well as the grated rind. Butter a 1-quart soufflé dish and put a layer of cornflakes on bottom of the dish. Add the cheese mixture and cover with another layer of cornflakes. Cover and refrigerate.

Before Serving

Preparation Time: 2 min.   *Cooking Time:* 1 hr.

Heat oven to 325°. Remove cover from soufflé dish and sprinkle brown sugar over the top. Bake, uncovered, for 1 hr. Allow to cool for 10 to 15 min. before serving. This pudding is also delicious cold and can, if you like, be baked the night before. We like it warm because it's the nearest thing to a soufflé we can think of for the cook who doesn't have much pre-dinner time in the kitchen. *Serves 6*

Strawberries with Vanilla Cream

1 pint fresh strawberries   1 quart boiling water
½ teaspoon vanilla

. . . .

Pressure can whipped cream

The Night Before

Preparation Time: 12 min.

While a quart of water is boiling, hull and wash the strawberries. Place in a colander in the sink and pour boiling water over the berries. Allow to cool slightly. Slice all but a few strawberries in half. Reserve 4 to 8 large, uncut berries. Place the cut berries in a bowl and sprinkle with vanilla. Cover and refrigerate. Put the reserved whole berries in a plastic bag and refrigerate.

Before Serving

Preparation Time: 2 to 3 min.

Add whipped cream to berries and mix gently but thoroughly. This should be done, if possible, about an hour before the dessert is served to give the cream and berry juice a chance to blend. Use the uncut berries for garnishing each portion. *Serves 4*

Mocha Almond Cream

1 cup sugar (superfine, if possible)   1 cup finely crushed almonds
½ lb. sweet butter, softened   4 oz. (4 squares) semi-sweet chocolate
¼ cup cherry or orange liqueur   ¼ cup strong coffee
¼ teaspoon almond extract   2 cups heavy cream, whipped

. . . .

Additional whipped cream for decoration (from a pressure can)

The Night Before

Preparation Time: 16 min.

Put coffee and chocolate in top of double boiler and cook until chocolate melts, while you start the other preparations. Cream sugar and softened butter until well blended. Using a rotary beater or an electric mixer, beat in liqueur and almond extract. Continue beating until sugar is so well dissolved that you can neither see it nor feel it. Beat in the crushed almonds (use your blender to pulverize the almonds), then fold in the melted chocolate. Refrigerate the mixture, so that the chocolate cools slightly, while you whip the cream. Fold in whipped cream. Spoon into individual dessert dishes and refrigerate.

Before Serving

Preparation Time: 1 min.

Although more whipped cream may seem superfluous, it is nice to squirt some pressurized whipped cream over this dessert to conceal its slightly choppy appearance. Don't cover it completely—just make a few artful lines to divert the eye.

Serves 8

Cheese Cake with Fruit Topping

1½ cups graham cracker crumbs (about 20 to 24 crackers)
¼ lb. (1 stick) butter or margarine, melted
3 tablespoons sugar
1 teaspoon vanilla
½ pint (1 cup) sour cream

12 oz. cream cheese, softened
¼ lb. farmer cheese
3 eggs, separated
¾ cup sugar
1 teaspoon vanilla
1 can pie filling (cherry, pineapple, strawberry, etc.)

The Night Before

Preparation Time: 18 min.   *Cooking Time:* 35 min.

(*Note:* Before starting any preparations, remove cream cheese from refrigerator and let it stand at room temperature to soften.)

Melt butter or margarine and mix with graham cracker crumbs (use blender to make crumbs, or buy a bag of graham cracker crumbs), 3 tablespoons sugar, and 1 teaspoon vanilla. Press crumb mixture into the bottom of an 8-inch spring form cake pan (about 2½ to 3 inches deep). Light oven so that it can preheat to 325°.

Put sour cream, softened cream cheese, farmer cheese, egg yolks, sugar, and vanilla in a large mixing bowl. Beat with an electric mixer or a rotary beater until mixture has a creamy consistency. Beat the three egg whites until stiff, then fold into cheese mixture. Pour this over the crust in the spring form pan. Bake at 325° for 35 min. Then, *without opening the oven*, turn the heat off; leave the cake in the unopened oven for another hour and a half. Then remove from oven, top with pie filling, and refrigerate.

When the cake is cold—either later that night or at any time before serving—remove the sides of the spring form pan.

Serves 8

Banana "Cream" Pie

The secret of this pie is time—24 hrs. in the refrigerator. And that's the kind of time we're most willing to give, isn't it? Speaking of time, the preparation time given below does not allow for rolling and baking a pie shell. There's no reason to roll your own, either, if your market stocks those ready-to-bake pie shells.

1 pint sour cream
4 egg yolks, lightly beaten
1 cup sugar
2 tablespoons plus 2 teaspoons cornstarch
1½ teaspoons vanilla
2 large or 3 small bananas
3 tablespoons lemon juice
Baked pie shell, 9 or 10 inches

For decorating the top (optional), any one of the following:
Cinnamon
Nutmeg
Fresh strawberries
Apricot preserves
Shaved chocolate
Whipped cream (add just before serving)

Preparation Time: 12 min.   *Cooking Time:* 20 min.

Bake pie shell according to instructions on package.

Heat sour cream in top of double boiler until thinned and heated through—do not allow it to get so hot that it curdles. While sour cream is heating, place egg yolks in large bowl, beat lightly, and add sugar and cornstarch. (This mixture will be lumpy and granular.)

Add heated sour cream to egg yolk mixture in bowl, pouring in a little at a time and stirring well after each addition. Return to top of double boiler and cook for 20 min. Remove from heat and stir in vanilla. Chill mixture for 30 min. or so.

When you are ready to assemble the pie, slice the bananas and spread them out, in one layer, on a dish. Pour lemon juice evenly over banana slices. Let stand for 2 or 3 min., then pour off lemon juice. Place a layer of sliced bananas on bottom of baked (and cooled) pie shell. Mix remaining bananas with chilled sour cream mixture and spoon into pie shell.

If you wish to decorate the pie (you don't *have* to) any of the following toppings will do beautifully:

A light sprinkling of cinnamon or nutmeg
A circle of strawberries around the outer edge
A light coating or an outer circle of apricot preserves
Shaved chocolate or chocolate curls
    (Any of the above may be added the night before)

Whipped cream—from an aerosol can, if you wish—added just
    before serving   *Serves 6 to 8*

Frozen Cream Cheese Cake Incognito

There is at least one very good brand of frozen cream cheese cake on the market. Although it is delicious, it's a rather plain-looking cake. This lack of decoration is a stroke of good fortune as far as we're concerned, because by adding just a little imagination to this basic cake you can create something that looks homemade and kind of special. We offer some suggestions just as a starter—take off from there according to your taste, imagination, and the contents of your pantry shelf.

The night before serving, partially thaw a frozen cream cheese cake (only the outer surface need be thawed). Decorate with:

Preserves—spread on sides and top

Jam and chopped nuts—spread jam over sides and top, then cover jam with chopped almonds, pecans, or walnuts

Pie filling—spoon over top

Jam or preserves and toasted coconut

Chocolate curls or shaved chocolate

Jam and fruit—spread a thin layer of apricot jam over top, then arrange well-drained canned peach halves, pineapple chunks, and apricot halves over jam

Return decorated, covered cake to refrigerator (not freezer).

Section Four

□ COMPANY DINNER #1 □

Dip de Luxe (page 103)   Vegetable Salad (page 81)
Boeuf Bourguignon (page 4)   Rolls
Noodles   Biscuit Tortoni (page 115)

The Night Before

Preparation Time: 55 min.   *Cooking Time:* 2½ hrs.

1. Brown the beef and get the Boeuf Bourguignon into the oven.
2. Prepare the Biscuit Tortoni and place, uncovered, in the freezer.
3. Chop one onion for the Dip de Luxe and, at the same time, slice one for the vegetable salad.
4. Open your cans of vegetables for the salad and let them drain in a colander in the sink while you prepare the dressing for marinating the salad. Transfer the drained vegetables and the sliced onion to a large bowl, pour the marinade over the vegetables, and refrigerate, covered.
5. Prepare the Dip de Luxe and refrigerate it in the dish in which you will serve it.
6. When the beef has cooked for the requisite 2½ hrs. and you put it in the refrigerator, cover the Biscuit Tortoni, which is already in the freezer, with aluminum foil at the same time.

Before Serving

Preparation Time: 10 min.   *Cooking Time:* 30 min.

At cocktail time: Serve the Dip de Luxe with potato chips.
40 min. before dinner: Heat oven to 325° for Boeuf Bour-

123

guignon. Put water and coffee in your coffeepot.

30 min. before dinner: Add mushrooms and onions and place Boeuf Bourguignon in oven. Set a large pot of water to boil for cooking the noodles.

12 min. before dinner: Put noodles in boiling water and cook for 10 to 12 min., according to package directions. At the same time you're in the kitchen to do this job, stir the Boeuf Bourguignon gently and replace in oven.

Just before serving: Pour marinade off vegetable salad. Drain noodles and place in a covered serving dish. Remove the beef casserole from the oven. Start the coffee just before you sit down at the table.

☐ COMPANY DINNER #2 ☐

Guacamole Nassau (page 103)   Biscuits (frozen)
Spicy Shrimp Dinner (page 38)   Banana "Cream" Pie (page 120)
Rice
Endive and Beet Salad (page
  79)

The Night Before

Preparation Time: 50 min.
          Cooking Time: 30 min. (in addition to preparation time)

1. Bake the pie shell. While it is baking, prepare the pie filling.
2. While the pie filling is cooking in the double boiler, begin the shrimp sauce. (Remember to remove the pie filling after it has cooked for 20 min. and to refrigerate it.)
3. When the shrimp sauce is simmering on the stove, prepare the Guacamole and refrigerate it.
4. Prepare the endive and refrigerate the uncut stalks in a plastic bag. Put the unopened can of beets in the refrigerator, too.
5. Remove pie filling from refrigerator. Fill the pie shell, decorate it, cover the pie with waxed paper or foil and refrigerate it.
6. Refrigerate the shrimp sauce.

Before Serving

Preparation Time: 12 min.   *Cooking Time:* 30 min.

There are so many ways of cooking rice and so many kinds of rice available that we haven't attempted to indicate where on this schedule you will start your rice cooking. Include this step according to the procedure for the type of rice you use.

Just for variety, we are suggesting that you serve the Guacamole as the first course after your guests are seated at the table. If you prefer, however, you can serve it with potato chips or crackers as an accompaniment to cocktails and then start dinner with the main course.

30 min. before dinner: Add shrimp, mushrooms, and okra to the sauce and put it on the stove to simmer. Cut the endive into 1-inch slices and place in the salad bowl with the drained beets. Pour salad oil and vinegar into cruets. Put water and coffee in coffeepot. Heat oven to 475° for the biscuits. Place biscuits on a cookie sheet.

5 min. before dinner: Place biscuits in oven. Mix Guacamole and place on individual serving dishes; garnish with parsley. Start coffee.

☐ COMPANY DINNER #3 ☐

Vegetable Soup (without meat
  balls) (page 112)
Veal Scallops Louise (page 26)
Pickled Peppers (page 85)
Baked Stuffed Mushrooms
  (page 91)

Italian bread sticks
Mocha Almond Cream (page
  118)

The Night Before

Preparation Time: 55 min.   *Cooking Time:* 30 min.

1. Take ½ lb. butter (for Mocha Almond Cream) from refrigerator and allow to stand at room temperature to soften.
2. Start to prepare vegetable soup.
3. While soup is coming to a boil, wash and seed peppers and
   set on stove to cook.
4. When soup has boiled, lower flame and simmer for 10 min.
   While soup is simmering, sprinkle veal with lemon juice,
   salt, and pepper. Prepare baked stuffed mushrooms.
5. Add pasta to soup. Simmer for an additional 10 min. while
   you complete Veal Scallops Louise and pickled peppers.
6. Prepare Mocha Almond Cream.
7. Refrigerate everything.

Before Serving

Preparation Time: 5 min.   *Cooking Time:* 20 min.

30 min. before dinner: Measure coffee and water into coffeepot.

20 min. before dinner: Put mushrooms in oven. Heat oven
to 350°. Pre-heat broiler.

10 min. before dinner: Put soup on stove to heat. Drain
peppers and place in serving dish. Put saucepan containing
lemon and butter mixture over very low heat to warm. Depending on thickness of veal, place in broiler 5 to 8 min. be-

fore serving. (If you have no device for keeping the veal warm while the soup course is being eaten, do not put veal in the broiler until the soup course has been served.) Start coffee.

Just before serving dessert: Decorate Mocha Almond Cream with pressurized whipped cream.

□ COMPANY DINNER #4 □

Marinated Shrimp (page 107)
Burgundy Pork Chops (page 31)
Hashed Brown Potatoes (page 87)

Cucumber and Laban Salad (page 78)
French bread
Cheese Pudding (page 117)

The Night Before
Preparation and Cooking Time: 1 hr., 20 min.

1. Peel and boil potatoes.
2. While potatoes are boiling, peel all onions and garlic you will need for the shrimp, potatoes, and salad.
3. Prepare shrimp and refrigerate.
4. Remove potatoes when done. While they are cooling, prepare Burgundy Pork Chops and refrigerate them.
5. Finish potatoes and refrigerate them.
6. Pare and dice cucumber and prepare salad. Refrigerate it.
7. Mix Cheese Pudding. Pour into soufflé dish and refrigerate.

Before Serving
Preparation Time: 12 min.   *Cooking Time: 1 hr.*

At cocktail time: Remove shrimp from marinade with a slotted spoon and serve in a bowl, with toothpicks for spearing.

75 min. before dinner: Heat oven to 325°.* Heat the Burgundy sauce on top of the stove. Pour over chops.

65 min. before dinner: Place pork chop casserole in oven. Sprinkle brown sugar on pudding.

60 min. before dinner: Place pudding in oven.

25 min. before dinner: Heat the skillet and fat for the

---

* The pork chops normally bake for 1 hr. at 350°. Since your oven will be set at 325° for the Cheese Pudding, you will be baking the chops 5 min. longer.

hashed brown potatoes. Put potatoes in pan to cook. Put water and coffee in coffeepot.

Just before serving: Slice French bread. Cut potatoes and remove to serving dish. Toss salad with laban. Start coffee. Remove pudding from oven and let it cool until dessert is served.

□ COMPANY DINNER #5 □

Chopped Liver (page 108)
Salmon Vinaigrette (page 44)
  with Parsley Mayonnaise
  (page 76)
Baked Stuffed Potatoes (page
  (88)

Vegetable Potpourri (page 92)
Brown and serve rolls
Cheese with fruit in season

The Night Before

Preparation Time: 55 min.   *Cooking Time:* 1 hr., 25 min.

1. Wash the potatoes and start them baking about half an hour before you plan to start your preparation of the dinner.
2. Peel and prepare onions needed for liver, salmon, and vegetable potpourri.
3. Cook liquid mixture for salmon steaks. While it is cooking, prepare vegetable potpourri and put it on the stove to simmer. By the time the salmon liquid is ready (after 25 min.), your potatoes can be removed from the oven, the temperature changed and the salmon can be put in the oven.
4. Put liver in pan to simmer.
5. By this time the potatoes will be cool enough to handle. Stuff and refrigerate them. Remove salmon from oven.
6. Prepare chopped liver and refrigerate it.
7. Cover and refrigerate salmon.
8. Prepare parsley mayonnaise and refrigerate it.
9. When vegetable potpourri is ready, cover and refrigerate it.

Before Serving

Preparation Time: 10 min.   *Cooking Time:* 20 min.

30 min. before dinner: Heat oven to 350°.

20 min. before dinner: Put potatoes, uncovered, in oven. Place chopped liver on individual serving dishes. Add salt, pepper, and capers to vegetable potpourri and set on stove to simmer. (Put brown and serve rolls in oven at appropriate time according to package directions.) Measure water and coffee into coffeepot. Arrange fruit and cheese on platter and let stand at room temperature.

Just before serving: Lift salmon from marinade and place on platter. Re-blend parsley mayonnaise and place in serving dish. Remove potatoes and rolls from oven. Start coffee.

☐ COMPANY DINNER #6 ☐

Mozzarella Appetizers (page 106)
Lamb Marengo (page 15)
Wild Rice Casserole (page 89)

Three-Way Eggplant (page 101)
Thinly sliced pumpernickel
Strawberries with Vanilla Cream (page 118)

The Night Before

Preparation Time: 1 hr.
Cooking Time: 50 min. (in addition to preparation time)

1. Heat oven to 475° and place eggplant in oven for 15 min.
2. Prepare Lamb Marengo. (While chopping the onion for the lamb, chop an extra quarter cup onion for the eggplant.) Put lamb on stove to simmer.
3. Peel eggplant and finish preparing it; refrigerate.
4. Boil water for strawberries.
5. Prepare wild rice casserole.
6. Complete preparation of strawberries.
7. Refrigerate both strawberries and rice casserole.
8. Prepare Mozzarella Appetizers and refrigerate.
9. When lamb has cooked for required time, cool and refrigerate.

Before Serving

Preparation Time: 12 min.   *Cooking Time:* 1 hr.

5 min. before cocktail time: Heat broiler and broil Mozzarella Appetizers for 2 min.

70 min. before dinner: Heat oven to 325°.

1 hr. before dinner: Put rice casserole in oven.

30 min. before dinner: Add mushrooms to Lamb Marengo and put on stove to simmer. Measure water and coffee into coffeepot. Mix strawberries and whipped cream and spoon into sherbet glasses or dessert plates and replace in refrigerator.

Just before serving: Pour any excess liquid off eggplant. Start coffee.

(In case you hadn't noticed, this menu makes economic sense. The wild rice and the dessert are fairly luxurious items, but their cost is balanced by the fact that you're using a very inexpensive—though delicious—cut of meat.)

□ COMPANY DINNER #7 □

Shrimp Toast (page 102.)
Chicken and Wild Rice (page 56)
Caesar Salad (page 77)

Oregano Bread Rounds (page 100.)
Cheese Cake with Fruit Topping (page 119.)

The Night Before

Preparation Time: 1 hr., 12 min.   *Cooking Time:* 1 hr., 15 min.

1. Start chicken simmering.
2. Take cream cheese (for cake) and butter (for bread rounds) from refrigerator to soften.
3. Start cooking wild rice.
4. Prepare Caesar Salad.
5. Heat oven to 325°. Prepare cheese cake and put it in oven to bake.
6. Prepare and refrigerate Shrimp Toast and Oregano Bread Rounds.
7. Turn oven off when cheese cake has baked for 35 min. Remove rice from stove when done.
8. Prepare onion, pimento, and mushrooms for chicken casserole.
9. When chicken is done and cooled enough to handle, complete preparation of the casserole and refrigerate it.
10. When cheese cake has been in turned-off oven for 1½ hrs., remove it. Spoon pie filling over top and refrigerate cake.

Before Serving

Preparation Time: 12 min.   *Cooking Time:* 30 min.

5 min. before cocktail time: Heat oil and fry shrimp toast.
40 min. before dinner: Heat oven to 350°.
30 min. before dinner: Stir chicken and rice casserole, add almonds and place, uncovered, in the oven. Put coffee and water into coffeepot.

10 min. before dinner: Put Oregano Bread Rounds in oven.

5 min. before dinner: Remove spring form from cheese cake.

Assemble Caesar Salad (unless you plan to do that at the table).

Start coffee.

□ COMPANY DINNER #8 □

Mushroom Biscuits (page 105)
Italian Veal with Tuna Sauce
  (page 25)
Caesar Green Beans (page 90)
Honeyed Carrots (page 89)

Parsley Buttered Bread (page
  99)
Pound Cake Pudding with Custard Sauce (page 115)

The Night Before

Preparation Time: 1 hr.   *Cooking Time:* 1¾ hrs.

1. Prepare veal and set on stove to simmer for 1¾ hrs.
2. Take ¼ lb. butter (for parsley-buttered bread) from refrigerator and let stand at room temperature to soften.
3. Heat oven to 350°. Soak pound cake crumbs (for pudding)
   in milk.
4. Scrape carrots. Put in pot with water. Bring to boil and
   simmer for 10 min.
5. Prepare Caesar Green Beans.
6. Add other ingredients to carrots after they have simmered
   for 10 min. Simmer for another 45 to 50 min.
7. Add other ingredients for pound cake pudding to the soaked
   crumbs. Put in oven for 1 hr.
8. Prepare and refrigerate mushroom biscuits, custard sauce,
   and the parsley buttered bread.
9. When veal is done, blend tuna sauce. Refrigerate veal and
   sauce.

Before Serving

Preparation Time: 11 min.   *Cooking Time:* 10 min.

15 to 20 min. before cocktail time: Preheat oven to temperature specified on biscuit package.

7 to 9 min. before cocktail time: Put mushroom biscuits in
oven.

20 min. before dinner: Heat oven to 350° for bread. Measure coffee and water into coffeepot.

10 min. before dinner: Put parsley buttered bread in oven. Start warming carrots. Melt butter and add butter and flour mixture to carrots. Drain beans, add other ingredients and put on stove to heat. While the beans and carrots are cooking (remember to stir the carrots occasionally), slice veal and place on serving platter. Put tuna sauce in serving dish. Slice pound cake pudding. When carrot liquid boils, lower flame and cook for 1 min. more while you remove green beans from heat and stir in cheese. Start coffee.

☐ COMPANY DINNER #9 ☐

Chicken Egg Drop Soup (page 110)
Tongue with Piquant Sauce (page 60)
Peas and Onions (page 97)

Mike's Cole Slaw (page 80)
Croissants
Frozen Cream Cheese Cake Incognito (page 121)

The Night Before

Preparation Time: 35 min.
    Cooking Time: 3 hrs. (will vary, depending on weight of tongue)

1. About an hour before starting dinner preparation, remove cream cheese cake from freezer and let stand at room temperature to thaw partially.
2. Peel and quarter onion and start tongue cooking.
3. Prepare piquant sauce for the tongue and put it on the stove to simmer for 10 min.
4. Wash and chop scallions for soup. Refrigerate.
5. Decorate cream cheese cake.
6. Remove piquant sauce from stove. Cool and refrigerate.
7. Prepare cole slaw.
8. When tongue is cooked, let it cool and then peel it. Cover and refrigerate.

Before Serving

Preparation Time: 10 min.   *Cooking Time:* 10 to 12 min.

30 min. before dinner: Slice tongue and arrange on serving platter. Put cole slaw in serving dish and replace in refrigerator. Put chicken broth in pot on stove but don't turn the heat on yet. Measure water and coffee into coffeepot.

10 min. before dinner: Cook frozen peas (or heat canned peas). Put chicken broth on stove to boil. Heat piquant sauce. Complete Chicken Egg Drop Soup and remove from heat. Mix peas with onions and butter. Pour soup into tureen or serving dishes and sprinkle with scallions. Start coffee.

☐ COMPANY DINNER #10 ☐

Antipasto (page 105)   Garlic Bread (page 100)
Mrs. Albini's Baked Lasagna   Vanilla ice cream with sweet
   (page 68)   liqueur
Italian Green Peppers (page 91)

The Night Before

Preparation Time: 55 to 60 min.   *Cooking Time:* 2 hrs., 45 min.

1. Prepare meat sauce for lasagna and simmer it for 2½ hrs.
2. Heat oven to 350°. Prepare roasted green peppers and bake for 35 to 40 min.
3. Prepare garlic bread and Antipasto and refrigerate these dishes and the roasted green peppers.
4. You can now take some time off. Come back into the kitchen to remove the peppers from the stove. Come back again half an hour before the meat sauce is due to be finished.
5. Boil water for lasagna. Go away and take another rest. Come back in about 20 min. When water has boiled, cook lasagna according to package directions. Heat oven to 350°.
6. Assemble lasagna in baking dish. Bake for 15 min.
7. Let lasagna stand for 15 min. after removing from oven. Cover and refrigerate. Refrigerate the meat separately in the top of a double boiler.

Before Serving

Preparation Time: 7 min.   *Cooking Time:* 20 min.

30 min. before dinner: Heat oven to 350°. Measure coffee and water into coffeepot.

20 min. before dinner: Put lasagna in oven. Put the meat in the top of the double boiler over hot water to warm.

10 min. before dinner: Put garlic bread in oven.

5 min. before dinner: Heat peppers in a saucepan on top of the stove.

Just before dinner: Start coffee. Remove lasagna from oven and let it stand for 5 or 10 min. before cutting.

Index

143